SLOW COOKER

RECIPES&PREPARATION

Publisher's Note: Raw or semi-cooked eggs should not be consumed by babies, toddlers, pregnant or breastfeeding women, the elderly or those suffering from a chronic illness.

Angela Litzinger: An expert in recipe development, Angela documents her family's meals and menus at angelaskitchen.com. When not puttering around the kitchen, hanging out with her husband and three kids (or the flock of sassy chickens in the back yard), she teaches food preservation and cooking clases, and contributes articles and recipes to numerous publications. The slow cooker is a treasured kitchen appliance, helping to get dinner on the table easily, giving her extra time to spend with her family no matter what their schedule looks like.

Publisher & Creative Director: Nick Wells
Senior Project Editor: Catherine Taylor
Copy Editor: Kathy Steer
Art Director: Mike Spender
Layout Design: Jane Ashley
Digital Design & Production: Chris Herbert
Proofreader: Dawn Laker

Special thanks to Amelia Edgell-Cole.

FLAME TREE PUBLISHING
6 Melbray Mews, Fulham,
London SW6 3NS, United Kingdom
www.flametreepublishing.com

This edition published 2017

Copyright © 2017 Flame Tree Publishing Ltd

17 19 21 20 18
1 3 5 7 9 10 8 6 4 2

ISBN: 978-1-78664-547-0

Picture Credits

© Crock-Pot®/Sunbeam Products, Inc.: 19br, 20r, 34t. © Morphy Richards: 19t. © Flame Tree Publishing: 143, 165. Courtesy **Shutterstock.com** and the following: 1 & 28l, 57, 176 MariaKovaleva; 3 & 198 mady70; 4 & 101 Lisovskaya Natalia; 6l, 9tl Iakov Filimonov; 6r Lesterman; 7l, 14bl, 29r Robyn Mackenzie; 7r zoryanchik; 9b sherwood; 9tr Syda Productions; 13tl, 14tl, 14tr, 21l, 34bl Kiian Oksana; 13b wavebreakmedia; 14br puhhha; 17t frantic00; 17b Y Photo Studio; 19bl Gaus Nataliya; 20l, 33bl Natasha Breen; 21r Olga Miltsova; 23 comeirrez; 24tl Barbara Dudzinska; 24br Grezova Olga; 27br, 33tl, 218 Africa Studio; 27t Ruslan Mitin; 27bl Vladeep; 28r Tatiana Volgutova; 29l DarZel; 30tl alexandre zveiger; 30b RazoomGame; 33br Elena Elisseeva; 33tr Lilyana Vynogradova; 34bl Alphonsine Sabine; 37 funnyangel; 47 Anna_Pustynnikova; 51 Brent Hofacker; 52 sarsmis; 54 Dionisvera; 59 Bernd Juergens; 63 Sentelia; 75 Viktor1; 80 All kind of people; 83 Anna Hoychuk; 87 ArtCookStudio; 95 NinaM; 97 Joshua Resnick; 99 Liliya Kandrashevich; 102 casanisa; 104 Angel Simon; 108 SEAGULL_L; 113 Anna Kurzaeva; 116 Lukas Gojda ; 125 Stepanek Photography; 135 hlphoto; 137 Aimee M Lee; 140 holbox; 147 Monkey Busines Images; 148 msheldrake; 152 5PH; 157 vm2002; 167 Goskova Tatiana; 170 Karissaa; 173 Anna_Pustynnikova; 184 marekuliasz; 192 vanillaechoes; 201 Onya; 207 ElenaKor; 208 Marina Nabatova; 211 Wiktory; 215 gkrphoto; 221 Elena Shashkina; 111, 115 naito29; 145, 155 Anna Shepulova; 179, 187 Sandhya Hariharan; 42, 212 Lucky_elephant; 60, 169 AS Food studio; 65, 217 MShev; 68, 107 Magdanatka; 93, 119 neil langan. © **StockFood** and the following: 13tr, 24tr, 24bl, 30tr, 197, 202 Eising Studio - Food Photo & Video; 41 Piga & Catalano s.n.c.; 45 Firmston, Victoria ; 48 Rose, Ludger; 67 Cogliantry, Michael; 71 Hoff, Dana; 76 People Pictures; 79 Hart, Michael; 85 Benjamins, Sven; 88 Young, Andrew; 120 Tolhurst, Charlotte; 123 Parissi, Lucy; 127 Wallace, Ian; 129 Keller & Keller Photography; 133 Gräfe & Unzer Verlag / Liebenstein, Jana; 151 Gregson, Jonathan; 159 & 224 Great Stock!; 160 Jones, Huw; 174 Crossland, Don; 180 Strokin, Yelena; 183 Crudo, George; 191 Cassidy, Peter; 188, 205 Janssen, Valerie.

SLOW COOKER

RECIPES&PREPARATION

Angela Litzinger

FLAME TREE
PUBLISHING

CONTENTS

INTRODUCING SLOW COOKERS

Most of us would love to have a home-cooked meal every night, not convenience meals or takeaways, but in today's busy world, it is hard to find the time or inclination to spend a lot of time in the kitchen. Welcome to the world of slow cookers (or 'crockpots', as they're also known, courtesy of the first company to make them), where food tastes flavourful and satisfying, is tender and succulent and, once the ingredients are prepared and in the pot, you can walk away and let the meal cook itself.

COMEBACK-CROCK

When most people think of slow cookers, they immediately think of the old gold, brown or avocado coloured crockpot that sat lonely on a shelf in the kitchen of

their childhood, never to be used except for the occasional dish. Well, times have changed, and the lowly crockpot is seeing a revival in today's kitchens.

So, what's so great about slow cooking anyway? That's an easy question to answer, even if all you've ever done is make a simple stew or chilli with your slow cooker. A slow cooker is extremely easy to use and food naturally tastes better when cooked slowly and evenly as in a slow cooker. Slow cooking not only ensures you have a hot meal prepared and ready to go on busy weeknight evenings, it can also leave the hob or oven available for other dishes during big meal gatherings.

USE ALL YEAR ROUND

Autumn and winter are always great seasons to use the slow cooker to make satisfying stews and roasts, but don't forget about it in the summer! It uses very little electricity

and won't overheat the house. Slow cookers can be used year round. I love that I can pull together the ingredients for a meal in the morning, put it all in the pot and then simply set it and walk away. The crockpot requires very little cleaning itself – yet another major reason slow cooking is so great.

The slow cooker has been a great tool to use with my kids when teaching them to cook. Have children layer the vegetables, add measured seasonings and start it up. They can sniff away at it all day, watching the magic changes happening through the lid.

As the day goes along, a slow cooker is busy cooking your meal for you. All you need to do when it is time to eat, depending on the recipe you have selected, is prepare a side dish or salad, add some bread, set the table and call the family in to eat. So simple and so satisfying!

THE WHYS & HOWS

WHY SLOW COOK?

personally love my slow cooker and use it 2–3 times a week. Slow cooking makes it possible to create healthy meals with a minimum of fuss, cooked and ready to go when I am ready to serve my family. There are so many reasons to add a slow cooker to your meal cooking line-up.

THE BENEFITS

Slow Cooking Saves Time

When using a slow cooker, you can go and do other things while your food cooks. Once you have the food prepared and placed in the crock, you don't have to stand around monitoring it. Unlike preparing food in an oven or on the hob, there's no boiling over or burning. One of the best things about a crockpot is that it doesn't require watching or stirring of food.

Slow Cooking Saves Money

Slow cookers can cut your grocery bill significantly by allowing you to buy less expensive cuts of meat, which naturally tenderize during the longer cooking time. I often save over 50 per cent on beef and chicken this way.

You can also save money by using a slow cooker to soak and cook dried beans, a saving of around 60 per cent over buying canned beans. (If using dried beans when a recipe calls for canned, roughly 150 g/5 oz/¾ cup of dried will equal a 400-g/15-oz can. They should be presoaked overnight – the 'regular' method – or put in a pot with water, brought to the boil, removed from the heat and left to soak for an hour – the 'quick' method. Or, dried beans take 6–8 hours to cook in a slow cooker, on Low. Remember that you should always boil kidney beans for 10 minutes prior to cooking, to break down harmful toxins in their skin.)

Slow Cooking Saves Energy

A slow cooker uses far less electricity to cook a roast than an oven does. A slow cooker can use around 250 watts of power, while an oven can draw up to 4000 watts, depending on what you're cooking and the model of oven. This works out to mean that a slow cooker operating for 7 hours will use only half the energy that an oven that is on for 1 hour, an energy saving of 50 per cent.

Slow Cooking is Healthy

Slow-cooked recipes rarely call for extra oils or fats since they use water or other liquids and time to cook the food. As long as you trim the fat from the meat, you will be serving a lower-fat meal then those prepared through frying. Foods cooked in slow cookers often retain more of their vitamins and minerals than foods that are fried or boiled due to being covered and cooked at a low, even temperature. Another advantage is that home-cooked meals can be made according to dietary needs (ie: lower-sodium, allergen-free, etc.) and thus will be tailored to your family's needs in a way that takeaway foods simply can't be.

Slow Cooking is Easy

Using a slow cooker is very easy: just layer your food into the crock, put on the lid, set it and walk away. It is seriously that simple. I set up my slow cooker in the morning before heading out and when I come home, dinner is done and ready to serve.

Slow Cooking Washing Up is Simple

Slow cookers allow you to cook an entire family meal in one dish, the crock. There is little fuss and minimal mess to clean afterwards. If your slow cooker has a removable crock, then cleaning is just that much easier. Removable crocks or inserts cut down on cleaning by allowing you to serve the meal in the crock itself and then easily wash it in a sink or dishwasher. Slow cookers with non-removable crocks should never be submerged in water, so clean the interiors of the slow cooker immediately after cooking for easier cleaning.

Slow-cooked Dishes are Tasty

Slow cookers improve the flavour of a meal by taking less expensive cuts of meat or simple beans and making them into tasty meals by simmering on a low heat and cooking for several hours, allowing flavours to meld and vegetables to become tender and infused with spices.

Slow Cooking Frees Up Cooking Space

Using a crockpot frees up your oven and hob for other cooking you may need to do. This is especially useful during the holidays when cooking for a crowd and every bit of extra cooking space is needed.

Slow Cooking Keeps Your Home Cool

Unlike ovens, a slow cooker will not heat up your kitchen. While it may be nice during the winter to have that extra boost of heat, it can be an altogether different story in the summer. Cooking with a slow cooker makes it possible to have many of your favourite normally oven-cooked meals without heating up the house on even the hottest of days.

CHOOSING YOUR SLOW COOKER

There are now a number of different makes and models of slow cookers available, in a large range of colours, shapes and sizes – from contemporary white and shiny stainless steel to dark, rustic earthenware, or a host of eye-catching bright, vibrant colours, guaranteed to brighten up any kitchen. Here are some factors to consider to help you find the perfect one for your kitchen, so you can happily use it for years to come.

SHAPE & FORM

Originally, slow cookers were only available as a round model, which were excellent for soups, stews and casseroles as well as puddings and cakes. However, slow cookers now come in an oval shape, which is perfect for small whole fish and joints of meat, such as a pot roast.

Whole chickens, brisket or ribs will also fit better in an oval shape, as do loaf pans, but if you're usually making beans or stews, shape doesn't matter as much, so buy the one that fits better in your cabinet or on your work surface.

Type of lid

All cookers have a heat-resistant lid, which is either ceramic, plastic or toughened glass; the latter – clear not opaque – is a much better option as it is ideal for seeing what is happening without lifting the lid. This is useful because, when using a slow cooker, you want to avoid opening the lid, since that lets out precious heat and thus extends cooking time.

FUNCTIONS

Removable Crock

It is possible to buy a slow cooker with a fixed inner cooking dish, but for more flexibility and ease of cleaning, look for a cooker with a removable dish, referred to in this book as the 'crock' or 'cooking dish'.

For even more flexibility, some slow cookers have a cooking dish that can be placed under the grill to brown the finished dish or can be used on the hob or in the oven.

Warm Setting

Slow cookers have both high- and low-temperature cooking settings, but some also come with a warming function, which keeps food warm for when you need it.

Timer

Some slow cookers also have built-in timers so that once the timer goes off, the slow cooker automatically switches to the warm setting. Unless you always plan to be home to turn off your slow cooker at the right time, having a built-in timer prevents food from overcooking.

SIZE

Coming in a good range of sizes, from 600 ml/1 pint/½ quart to 6.5 litres/11½ pints/5¾ quarts, there is a slow cooker to suit every requirement. There are even slow cookers that come with more that one crock, each of a different size.

When choosing your cooker, think about the type of dishes you will be cooking, how many people you will be serving and how often you will use your cooker. If you feel that you would like to use the cooker nearly every day and you will be cooking for the

whole family, it makes sense to buy a larger cooker – one that you can use to its full potential. Most slow-cooker recipes are written for slow cookers between 4.5–7 litres/8–12 pints/4–6 quarts. The key to size is that slow cookers need to be at least half full to get the best results.

How Many People Are You Cooking For?

Here's a rough guide to help you decide which size you need:

- 4 litre/7 pint/3½ quart serves a 2–3 person household

- 4.5 litre/8 pint/4 quart serves 2 with leftovers for lunch the next day, or serves 4

- 6 litre/10½ pint/5 quart serves 4–6

- 7 litre/12 pint/6 quart serves 6–8, and is useful for doubling recipes for large batches

USiNG YOUR SLOW COOKER

All cookers have a low wattage, whatever their size. Normally, they have four settings: high, low, warm and off. Cooking on high for 2½ hours is equal to 1 hour's conventional cooking. If the recipe states 'low', it can generally be left on low for 8–9 hours to cook so that you can go out and have your meal waiting for you on your return.

LOW VS. HiGH

Check the instruction booklet for specific guidelines for the model you own. Slow cookers with a countdown timer will automatically switch over to 'warm' until you are ready to eat after the allotted cooking time is complete.

Some foods, such as poultry, cakes and most puddings, should be cooked on high for at least the first hour, then they can be turned to auto (medium) if preferred, or according to the manufacturer's instructions or recipe guidelines.

At the low setting, the food will just simmer, which is ideal for soups and casseroles. At high, the temperature is just below boiling, so is perfect for poultry. At auto (medium), the cooker will gradually build up to high, then cook for 1 hour before automatically switching to low for the rest of the cooking time.

If you have an older slow cooker and have purchased a new one, be aware newer models run hotter than they did even 10 years ago. The 'low' setting runs almost as hot as the 'hot' setting on old models. This was changed to standardize the heat settings across various models due to safety concerns and for consistency for recipe instruction.

THINGS TO REMEMBER

Fill the slow cooker one-half to three-quarters of the way full. Instructions will vary for cakes, puddings, breads and items cooked in a water bath, so follow the instructions in those recipes for best results.

- Make sure you are at home the first time you use your slow cooker. Just like any appliance, you need to make sure it's working properly during its first use.

- The outside of the slow cooker gets warm. Clear the area around the slow cooker so that nothing is touching the outside of the cooker while it is on.

- Once the lid is placed on the slow cooker, don't remove it any more often than the recipe states. Every time a lid is removed, heat and moisture escape and 15 minutes of cooking time will need to be added.

Place Your Slow Cooker in a Safe Location

Set your slow cooker on a heat-resistant surface, away from draughts and well away from the edge of the work surface where, small children and pets can't reach.

PREPARING & COOKING FOODS

PLANNING & TIMING

A few simple tips are the key to creating a rich, satisfying slow-cooked meal. As is often the way in life, you get the best results when you plan a little before diving in. So get to know your slow cooker and bear in mind the following advice.

Preheat or Not?

Some slow cookers need to be preheated before use, while others advise against heating the cooker with nothing in it, so double-check the manufacturer's instructions. Before preheating, most manufacturers advise that a small amount of cold water,

about 2.5cm/1 inch, should be poured into the cooking dish. By doing this, when boiling water is later added, there is no harm done to the cooker through the shock of temperature changes, as the dish is already warm. Slow cookers can be filled to within 2–3 cm/¾–1¼ inches of the top.

Don't Use Frozen Food

Loading a slow cooker with frozen ingredients will keep food in the danger zone where bacteria can flourish (4–60°C/40–140°F). Make sure your meat and vegetables are thawed before turning the cooker on.

Keep the Lid Closed

Each un-called-for peek you take during the cooking process will add an extra 15–20 minutes of cooking time. Curb the urge to stir; it's usually not necessary and tends to slow down the cooking.

Set the Heat Level

A general rule of thumb is that cooking on the low setting (77°C/170°F for most models) takes about twice as long as cooking on high (138°C/280°F on most models). Keep in mind that some cuts of meat and recipes are better suited to one setting over the other.

Adjust for High Altitude

For high-altitude cooking, add an extra 30 minutes for each hour of time specified in the recipe. Legumes take about twice as long as they would at sea level.

FOR BEST RESULTS

Choose the Right Cut of Meat

Chuck roasts, short ribs, pork shoulders and lamb shanks (think fatty and tougher meats) become meltingly tender with the moist, low heat of a slow cooker. Leaner cuts like pork fillet (tenderloin) tend to dry out. Likewise, dark meat chicken, such as thighs and drumsticks, will remain juicier and have better texture than white meat breasts.

Trim Fat

Take a minute or two and cut the excess fat from meat. Skip this step and you risk ending up with oily cooking liquid as any fat does not drain from the dish. When possible, remove chicken skin as well.

Browning Boosts Taste

You can certainly just pile food into the slow cooker, turn it on and get tasty results. But when you take a couple of minutes to brown meat or caramelize vegetables before adding them to the crock, you're rewarded with an additional layer of flavour. Want a thicker sauce? Dredge the meat in flour or cornflour (cornstarch) before browning. As far as minced (ground) meat is concerned, always precook and drain mince (ground meat) before adding to a slow cooker.

Avoid Overcrowding

For the best results, fill a slow cooker between one-half and two-thirds full. Go ahead and cook large roasts and whole chickens, making sure to use a large crock with a lid that fits snugly on top.

Layer Wisely

For even cooking, cut food into uniformly sized pieces. Place firm, slow-cooking root vegetables such as potatoes and carrots at the bottom of the crock and place the meat on top.

Watch the Wine

Because the cooker is sealed, the alcohol in wine doesn't evaporate out as it does in a regular pot or frying pan.

Add Dairy Last

Sour cream, milk and yogurt tend to break down and curdle in the slow cooker, so stir them in during the last 15 minutes of cooking. This also applies to any dairy-free alternatives.

End on a Fresh Note

A sprinkle of fresh herbs or a squeeze of lemon juice at the end of simmering can brighten flavours of long-cooked recipes. Other excellent finishing touches include citrus zest, hot sauce, grated Parmesan or a drizzle of olive oil.

CARE OF YOUR SLOW COOKER

While slow cookers seem similar across the different brands, it is always wise to read the manufacturer's booklet to learn about your appliance and its features. Slow cookers even from the same manufacturer do vary, so it is important that you understand your cooker before using it.

Clean Before Using

Remove all the packaging from a new slow cooker. Wash the cooking dish and lid in warm, soapy water, rinse and dry.

BEST PRACTICE

Don't Shock the Crock

The ceramic insert in a slow cooker can crack if exposed to abrupt temperature shifts. In other words, don't place a hot ceramic insert directly on a cold work surface; put down a dish towel first. The same goes for using a filled insert you've stowed overnight in the refrigerator: let it come to room temperature before putting it in a preheated base.

Unplug after Use

Always switch the cooker off on the control button and unplug after using.

Clean Straight Away

Empty completely and allow to cool. Wash the cooking dish in hot, soapy water. Soaking the *inside* of the cooking dish if necessary to remove any stubborn food.

However, do not leave the base of the cooking dish soaking in water – part of the dish is unglazed and soaking can damage it.

Electricity & Water Don't Mix

Never immerse the base of the cooker itself in water. It is an electrical appliance and so the electric elements should be kept away from water. Wipe the outside with a damp cloth, if needed.

EASY CLEANING TIPS FOR COOKED-ON FOODS

Soak on Low

Fill the slow cooker with water and set to cook on low for 2 hours. A low-heat soak for a few hours is the easiest, hands-off way to deep-clean your slow-cooker insert.

Soda Sparkle

For more persistent stains, add a few tablespoons of bicarbonate of soda (baking soda) and a few drops of washing-up liquid (dishwashing soap) to the water before turning the setting to low. After a few hours, pour away the water and wipe down the insert with a little more soda and a non-scratch pad.

Vanish with Vinegar

Black slow-cooker inserts sometimes develop a white film from mineral deposits. The film won't affect the cooking, but you can get rid of it with vinegar. Fill the crock with water, add 250 ml/8 fl oz/1 cup white vinegar, then allow to soak for a few hours or overnight. Wash and dry as usual.

SOUPS, SIDES & SNACKS

CREAMY CARROT SOUP

Warm and comforting, this creamy carrot soup is especially delicious on a chilly evening. If the soup is too thick after adding the cream, thin with small amounts of stock or a bit more cream until the desired consistency is reached.

Serves 8

1.3 kg/3 lb carrots (about 15), peeled and chopped

2 onions, peeled and chopped

2 large Russet potatoes, peeled and chopped

2 tbsp olive oil

2 garlic cloves, peeled and very finely chopped

½ tsp dried thyme

½ tsp dried marjoram

1.5 litres/2½ pints/6 cups vegetable or chicken stock

50 ml/2 fl oz/¼ cup cream or canned coconut milk

2 tbsp honey

½ tsp freshly grated nutmeg, plus extra if needed

sea salt and freshly ground black pepper

Combine the carrots, onions, potatoes, olive oil, garlic, herbs and stock in the cooking dish of a 7 litre/12 pint/6 quart slow cooker. Cover and cook on High for 3½–4 hours or on Low for 7–8 hours until the vegetables are soft.

Purée in batches in a food processor or blender or with a hand-held stick (immersion) blender in the slow cooker. Stir in the cream, honey and nutmeg, then season with salt and pepper.

TOMATO & BASIL SOUP

Sweet, summery tomato flavour pairs beautifully with basil in this classic soup.

Serves 8

3 large carrots, peeled and chopped

2 celery stalks, diced

2 sweet onions, peeled and chopped

4 garlic cloves, peeled and left whole

2 tsp salt, plus extra to taste

¼ tsp freshly ground black pepper

2.8 kg/6 lb/13⅔ cups canned whole peeled tomatoes, or 3.6 kg/8 lb fresh plum
   tomatoes peeled and seeded

1 litre/1¾ pints/4 cups chicken or vegetable stock

5–15 g/¼–½ oz/¼–½ cup fresh basil leaves, roughly chopped, plus extra to garnish

single cream (half and half), double (heavy) cream or canned coconut milk (optional)

Place all the ingredients except the cream into the cooking dish of a 7 litre/12 pint/6 quart slow cooker. Cover and cook on High for 4 hours or Low for 7–8 hours. The vegetables should be very soft.

Use a hand-held stick (immersion) blender to purée the soup. Alternatively, work in batches and puree the soup in a blender (only partially fill the blender, or it will splatter and escape from the lid). If using fresh tomatoes, the soup may be a bit thin. If so, cook on High for 30 minutes or 1 hour on Low with the lid off until you reach the desired thickness.

When ready to serve, stir in the cream. Taste and add more salt and pepper, if needed. Ladle into bowls and sprinkle with extra basil and freshly ground black pepper.

TOMATO & CHICKPEA SOUP

This flavourful, hearty soup is loaded with chickpeas and vegetables. If you like extra veggies, stir in 150 g/5 oz/3 cups chopped fresh kale or spinach 30 minutes before the end of cooking time.

Serves 8

1 tbsp olive oil

2 carrots, peeled and diced

2 celery stalks, diced

1 onion, peeled and chopped

4 garlic cloves, peeled and very finely chopped

1.2 kg/2¾ lb/4½ cups canned chickpeas, rinsed and drained

700 g/1½ lb/3½ cups canned whole tomatoes, crushed with hands

700 g/1½ lb/3½ cups canned whole tomatoes, sliced in half

1 litre/1¾ pints/4 cups chicken or vegetable stock

2 fresh rosemary sprigs

3 bay leaves

salt and freshly ground black pepper

4 tbsp freshly chopped basil, to garnish

Heat the oil in a frying pan over a medium-high heat. Add the carrots, celery, onion and garlic and sauté for 6–8 minutes until tender and fragrant. Transfer the vegetables to the cooking dish of a 7 litre/12 pint/6 quart slow cooker. Stir in the chickpeas, tomatoes, stock, rosemary and bay leaves. Cover and cook on Low for 6 hours.

Remove the bay leaves and rosemary sprigs and season to taste with salt and black pepper. Sprinkle with chopped basil and serve.

PUMPKIN & COCONUT SOUP

Pumpkin soup is one of my favourite soups to make every autumn. It's wonderful for lunch or supper!

Serves 8

2 tbsp olive oil

1 large onion, peeled and chopped

4 large carrots, peeled and chopped

2 celery stalks, chopped

4 garlic cloves, peeled and very finely chopped

1 tbsp curry powder

1 tsp ground cumin

1 tsp ground cardamom

1 tsp ground coriander

¼ tsp cayenne pepper, or to taste

⅛ tsp ground nutmeg

salt and freshly ground black pepper

1 tbsp light brown sugar

575 g/1¼ lb/2⅓ cups canned pumpkin purée

1.5 litres/2½ pints/6 cups vegetable or chicken stock

400 ml/14 fl oz/1⅔ cups canned full-fat coconut milk

TO GARNISH (OPTIONAL)

40 g/1½ oz/⅓ cup roasted salted pumpkin seeds

15 g/½ oz/¼ cup chopped coriander (cilantro)

15 g/½ oz/1½ cups toasted croutons

275–425 g/10–15 oz/2–3 cups shredded cooked chicken

Heat the oil in a large nonstick frying pan over a medium heat. Add the onion, carrots, and celery and cook for about 10 minutes until tender. Add the garlic, spices and a dash of salt and black pepper. Cook for about 2 minutes, stirring constantly. Transfer the mixture to the cooking dish of a 7 litre/12 pint/6 quart slow cooker.

Add the brown sugar, pumpkin purée and stock. Stir and cook on High for 4 hours, or on Low for 8 hours.

Once the soup has cooked, stir in the coconut milk, then purée the soup either with a hand-held stick (immersion) blender or in a blender, in batches.

Keep the soup warm in your slow cooker until you are ready to serve. Serve the soup on its own or with the garnishes.

MINESTRONE SOUP

Minestrone soup can be made with pasta or rice, depending on how you like it. Whichever way you stir it up, it's delicious!

Serves 8

4 carrots, peeled and chopped

3 medium potatoes, peeled and chopped

3 celery stalks, chopped

425 g/15 oz tomatoes, diced

1 onion, peeled and diced

4 garlic cloves, peeled and very finely chopped

1½ tbsp Italian seasoning

1 tsp salt

½ tsp ground black pepper

2 bay leaves

1 litre/1¾ pints/4 cups vegetable, chicken or beef stock

500 ml/18 fl oz/2 cups water

750 ml/1¼ pints/3¼ cups tomato juice

425 g/15 oz/2½ cups canned red kidney beans, drained and rinsed

425 g/15 oz/2½ cups canned cannellini beans, drained and rinsed

175 g/6 oz/1½ cups courgettes (zucchini), diced

200 g/7 oz/1½ cups fresh or frozen chopped green beans or chopped broccoli

100 g/3½ oz/1 cup uncooked pasta of choice, such as dittalini, or white long-grain rice

grated Parmesan, to serve (optional)

Stir together all the ingredients, except the courgettes (zucchini), green beans and pasta, in the cooking dish of a 7 litre/12 pint/6 quart slow cooker. Cover and cook on High for 3–4 hours or on Low for 6–8 hours.

Stir in the courgettes, green beans and pasta. Cover and cook on High for 20–30 minutes until the pasta is tender. Serve with grated Parmesan, if desired.

CREAMY WILD RICE
& Chicken Soup

This creamy soup is studded with chicken, vegetables and nutty wild rice.

Serves 8

2 litres/3½ pints/8 cups chicken stock

450 g/1 lb cooked chicken, chopped

225 g/8 oz mushrooms, sliced

1 onion, peeled and finely chopped

2 carrots, peeled and sliced

1 celery stalk, chopped

100 g/3½ oz/½ cup uncooked wild rice

100 g/3½ oz/½ cup uncooked long-grain rice

2 tbsp olive oil

1 tbsp dried parsley

1 garlic clove, peeled and very finely chopped

½ tsp salt

½ tsp ground black pepper

½ tsp curry powder

200 ml/7 fl oz/¾ cup water

6 tbsp cornflour (cornstarch)

250 ml/8 fl oz/1 cup canned coconut milk

Place all the ingredients, except the water, cornflour (cornstarch) and coconut milk, in the cooking dish of a 7 litre/12 pint/6 quart slow cooker. Cover and cook on Low for 6 hours.

Stir the water and cornflour together in a small bowl, then pour into the soup with the coconut milk. Cover and turn to High. Cook for 20–30 minutes until thickened. Stir and serve.

GLAZED CARROTS

Slow cookers aren't just for casseroles – try using yours to make this tasty side dish. If you can't get baby carrots, use large carrots instead. Just peel them and chop into thirds.

Serves 6-8

900 g/2 lb baby carrots, peeled
100 g/3½ oz/½ cup (packed) soft brown sugar, honey or orange marmalade
2 tbsp butter or coconut oil
½ tsp salt, or to taste
1 tbsp freshly chopped parsley, to garnish

Oil the cooking dish of a 4–4.5 litre/7–8 pint/3½–4 quart slow cooker. Place the baby carrots in the dish with the brown sugar, butter and salt. Mix well, cover and cook on High for 4–5 hours, stirring after 2 hours. Cook until the carrots are tender.

Stir the carrots and sprinkle with parsley before serving.

WARM CURRIED POTATO SALAD

This is a spicy, fragrant take on a summer classic.

Serves 10–12

1.3 kg/3 lb salad (fingerling) potatoes, halved lengthways

200 ml/7 fl oz/¾ cup chicken stock

3 garlic cloves, peeled and very finely chopped

1 tsp ground turmeric

1 tsp mild chili powder, or to taste

1 tsp salt

½ tsp ground cinnamon

½ tsp ground cumin

½ tsp ground black pepper

300 g/11 oz/1⅓ cups mayonnaise, plain full-fat Greek-style yogurt, or half of each

2 tsp freshly grated root ginger

1 tbsp freshly chopped coriander (cilantro)

Place the potatoes in the cooking dish of a 4.5–7 litre/8–12 pint/4–6 quart slow cooker. Stir in the stock, garlic, turmeric, chili powder, salt, cinnamon, cumin and pepper. Cover and cook on High for 3½–4 hours until the potatoes are tender, stirring once during cooking. Remove the potatoes with a slotted spoon, reserving 100 ml/3½ fl oz/⅓ cup of the cooking liquid.

Mix the mayonnaise or yogurt, ginger, coriander (cilantro) and the reserved cooking liquid together in a bowl.

Mix the dressing with the potatoes and leave to stand for 5 minutes before serving.

CHEESE FONDUE

Creamy, stretchy fondue is a fun dip for any party!

Serves 20 as a starter (appetizer)

750 ml/1¼ pints/3 cups reduced-salt chicken stock

750 ml/1¼ pints/3 cups double (heavy) cream

250 ml/8 fl oz/1 cup dry white wine

3 garlic cloves, peeled and very finely chopped

125 g/4 oz/½ cup butter, room temperature

65 g/2½ oz/½ cup plain (all-purpose) flour, or 4 tbsp cornflour (cornstarch)

FLAVOUR OPTIONS

Classic

450 g/16 oz/4 cups grated Swiss cheese

225 g/8 oz/2 cups grated Emmenthal (Emmentaler)

1 tbsp Dijon mustard

Blue

450 g/16 oz/4 cups grated Gruyère cheese

225 g/8 oz/1⅔ cups crumbled blue cheese

2 tbsp honey

Herbed

450 g/16 oz/4 cups grated Havarti

225 g/8 oz/1 cup semi-soft cheese of choice

1 tbsp Herbs de Provence seasoning

1 tsp finely chopped lemon zest

Combine the stock, cream, wine and garlic in the cooking dish of a 4.5 litre/8 pint/4 quart slow cooker. Cover and cook on Low for 4–5 hours.

Mix the butter and flour together in a small bowl until a paste forms. Stir the butter mixture into the stock mixture until combined. Cover and cook on Low for a further 30 minutes.

Whisk the flavour options into the stock until smooth. Serve with assorted dippers, such as bread cubes, steamed vegetables, etc.

CLASSIC HUMMUS

You can make homemade hummus simply and at a big discount using your slow cooker. Delicious!

Serves 10-12 starter (appetizer) servings

250 g/9 oz/1½ cups dried chickpeas, rinsed

50 ml/2 fl oz/¼ cup olive oil

50 ml/2 fl oz/¼ cup lemon juice

2 tsp very finely chopped garlic

1 tsp salt

¼ tsp ground black pepper

TO GARNISH

paprika, for sprinkling

freshly chopped parsley

Place the chickpeas in the cooking dish of a 4.5 litre/8 pint/4 quart slow cooker and add enough water to cover 5 cm/2 inches above the top of the beans. Cover and cook on High for 4–5 hours or 8–10 hours on Low until the chickpeas are very soft and easily mashed. Check the water level occasionally; if water looks low, add more hot water.

When the chickpeas are very soft, remove them with a slotted spoon and place in a food processor or blender, reserving the cooking liquid. Add the olive oil, lemon juice, garlic, salt, black pepper and 100 ml/3½ fl oz/⅓ cup of the leftover cooking liquid to the chickpeas in the food processor or blender and pulse until smooth. If needed, add more cooking liquid 1 tablespoon at a time until the hummus is at the desired consistency.

Allow to cool covered in the refrigerator before serving, garnished with paprika and parsley.

CHICKEN LIVER PÂTÉ

Using a slow cooker is a great way to make homemade pâté as baking in an oven can often dry it out. That will not happen in the slow cooker. You can use this recipe as a general guideline, altering the flavourings and spices to suit your tastes.

Serves 12 as a starter (appetizer)

600 g/1 lb 5 oz chopped chicken livers

1 onion, peeled and chopped

200 g/7 oz/¾ cup plus 2 tbsp butter

salt and freshly ground black pepper

2 garlic cloves, peeled and finely chopped

3 tbsp brandy

1 tsp thyme or sage

Fry the liver and onion in 15 g/½ oz/1 tablespoon of the butter in a frying pan with salt and pepper to taste. After 3 minutes, add the garlic and cook for a further 2 minutes. Stir in the brandy and ignite it to evaporate the alcohol. Stir in the remaining butter and the thyme or sage. Leave or pulse in a food processor if your prefer a smoother pâté.

Transfer the pâté to a well-greased terrine dish, cover it tightly with greased foil and put it in the cooking dish of a 4.5 litre/8 pint/4 quart slow cooker.

Pour enough water into the cooking dish to come halfway up the terrine dish. Cover and cook on Low for 9–10 hours.

STICKY CHICKEN WINGS

These amazing chicken wings take only take 5 minutes to prepare with no deep-frying! They're sticky, slightly sweet and perfect as a starter or main dish.

Serves 6 or 10 as a starter (appetizer)

100 ml/3½ fl oz/⅓ cup reduced-salt soy sauce (gluten-free if needed)

100 ml/3½ fl oz/⅓ cup balsamic vinegar

75 g/3 oz/⅓ cup (packed) soft brown sugar

75 g/3 oz/¼ cup honey

3 garlic cloves, peeled and very finely chopped

1 tsp sriracha sauce, or more to taste

1 tsp ground ginger

1 tsp ground black pepper

½ tsp onion powder

1½ tbsp sesame seeds, to garnish

FOR THE CHICKEN WINGS

1.3 kg/3 lb chicken wings

2 tbsp cornflour (cornstarch)

Whisk the soy sauce, vinegar, sugar, honey, garlic, sriracha, ginger, pepper and onion powder together in a small bowl.

Place the wings into the cooking dish of a 7 litre/12 pint/6 quart slow cooker. Pour over the soy sauce mixture and gently stir to combine. Cover and cook on High for 1–2 hours or Low for 3–4 hours.

Whisk the cornflour (cornstarch) and 2 tablespoons water together in a small bowl.

Stir the mixture into the slow cooker. Cover and cook on High for a further 10–15 minutes until the sauce has thickened.

Preheat the grill (broiler) and line a baking sheet with foil or baking parchment. Place the wings onto the prepared baking sheet and grill (broil) for 2–3 minutes until caramelized and slightly charred. Serve immediately with any remaining sauce, garnished with sesame seeds.

CORNMEAL SPOONBREAD

Soft, fluffy and delicious, this spoonbread is incredible as a side for an autumn meal.

Serves 6

175 g/6 oz/1 cup polenta (cornmeal)

about 600 ml/1 pint/2½ cups whole milk or unsweetened almond milk

4 tbsp unsalted butter or coconut oil

325 g/11½ oz/2 cups sweetcorn kernels, fresh, or thawed if frozen

2 tbsp granulated sugar

1 tsp salt

⅛ tsp cayenne pepper

3 medium (large) eggs, separated

¼ tsp cream of tartar

Oil the cooking dish of a 2.3 litre/4 pint/2 quart slow cooker. Set aside.

Whisk the polenta (cornmeal) and 200 ml/7 fl oz/¾ cup milk in a bowl until combined; set aside.

Melt the butter in a frying pan over a medium-high heat. Add the sweetcorn kernels and cook for 3 minutes, or until they are beginning to brown. Stir in the remaining milk and the sugar, salt and cayenne pepper and bring to the boil. Remove from the heat, cover and let the mixture steep for 15 minutes.

Transfer the warm sweetcorn mixture to a blender or food processor and purée until smooth, then pour into a pan and bring to the boil. Reduce the heat to low and add the polenta mixture, whisking constantly for 2–3 minutes until thickened. Transfer to a large bowl and cool to room temperature, about 20 minutes. Once cooled, whisk in the egg yolks until combined.

With an electric mixer on medium-low speed, beat the egg whites and cream of tartar until frothy, about 1 minute. Increase the speed to medium-high and beat until stiff peaks form, about 3 minutes. Whisk one-third of the whites into the corn mixture, then gently fold in the remaining whites until combined. Scrape the mixture into the prepared cooking dish.

Cover and cook on High for 2–3 hours or on Low for 4–5 hours. Spoonbread is ready when the centre is set and an inserted skewer comes out clean.

BAKED SWEET POTATO
With Feta Cheese & Chives

'Bake' sweet potatoes easily in your slow cooker without heating up your kitchen.

Serves 4

4 medium sweet potatoes or yams, scrubbed and dried

TO SERVE

75 g/3 oz/½ cup feta, crumbled
5 g/⅛ oz/¼ cup freshly chopped chives
salt and freshly ground black pepper

Using a fork, poke holes in the sweet potato 3 or 4 times.

Wrap each sweet potato in foil and place in the cooking dish of a 7 litre/12 pint/6 quart slow cooker. Cover and cook on Low for 8 hours, or until tender.

Mix the topping ingredients together in a bowl. Cut the potatoes in half, add the topping and serve.

Note:

Serve the sweet potatoes with tasty toppings, such as butter and brown sugar with cinnamon, or maple syrup with crisp bacon. If you prefer crisper skins, cut the sweet potatoes in half before topping and pop skin-side up under the grill (broiler) for 2 minutes. Watch closely so they do not scorch.

BOSTON BROWN BREAD
with Raisins

Dark, slightly sweet Boston Brown Bread pairs perfectly with baked beans and hot dogs for an authentically Bostonian meal.

Makes 4 small loaves

130 g/4½ oz/1 cup wholemeal (wholewheat) flour

100 g/3½ oz/1 cup rye flour

175 g/6 oz/1 cup polenta (cornmeal)

1 tsp bicarbonate of soda (baking soda)

⅛ tsp salt

500 ml/18 fl oz/2 cups buttermilk

250 g/9 oz/¾ cup molasses

2 tbsp soft brown sugar

75 g/3 oz/½ cup raisins, chopped

Mix the flours, polenta (cornmeal), bicarbonate of soda (baking soda) and salt in a large bowl to combine. Make a well in the centre of the dry ingredients, add the buttermilk, molasses, brown sugar and raisins and stir until everything is just combined.

Lightly grease 4 wide-mouthed, straight-sided, 600 ml/1 pint canning jars and their lids. Divide the batter among the jars, filling about two-thirds of the way up. Place the lids on the jars loosely. Transfer to the cooking dish of a 7 litre/12 pint/6 quart slow cooker and fill the cooker with enough water to reach the batter line in the jars. Cover and cook on High for 2½ hours, or until cooked through (when there is no batter on a skewer pushed into the bread).

Remove the jars from the slow cooker and rest until cool enough to handle. Remove the lids, then shake the jars gently to remove the bread. Let them finish cooling on a wire rack.

FISH & SEAFOOD

WHOLE BAKED FISH

This is a beautifully aromatic dish with a fantastic presentation. You will need a large slow cooker to cook a whole fish of this size. Otherwise, cut off the head and tail before cooking.

Serves 8

1.25 kg/2½ lb whole salmon, trout or small salmon, cleaned (and trimmed to fit, if necessary)

sea salt and freshly ground black pepper

50 g/2 oz butter or coconut oil

1 garlic clove, peeled and finely sliced

grated zest and juice of 1 lemon

grated zest of 1 orange

1 tsp freshly grated nutmeg

3 tbsp Dijon mustard

2 tbsp fresh white breadcrumbs

2 bunches fresh dill

1 bunch fresh tarragon

1 lime, sliced

150 ml/¼ pint/⅔ cup half-fat crème fraîche

450 ml/¾ pint/1¾ cups fromage frais

dill sprigs and lime or orange slices, to garnish

Lightly rinse the fish and pat dry. Season the cavity with salt and pepper. Make diagonal cuts across the flesh of the fish and season.

Mix the butter, garlic, lemon and orange zest and lemon juice, nutmeg, mustard and breadcrumbs together in a bowl. Spoon the breadcrumb mixture into the slits along with a small sprig of dill. Place the remaining herbs inside the fish cavity and lay the fish on a double thickness of nonstick baking parchment. Top with the lime slices and fold the paper into a parcel.

Place in the cooking dish of a 7 litre/12 pint/6 quart slow cooker and switch to High. Cover with the lid and cook for 30 minutes, then switch to Low and cook for 3–4 hours until the fish is cooked through.

To test if the fish is cooked, insert a skewer into the thickest part of the fish; if it yields easily with no resistance, it is cooked. Remove the fish from the cooker and leave to stand for 10 minutes. Stir the crème fraîche and fromage frais into the fish juices in the dish. Switch to High and cook for 15–20 minutes, stirring occasionally. Garnish and serve immediately.

CHUNKY FISH STEW

This simple fish stew is a refreshing change from the usual beef stew – hearty
and delicious.

Serves 6-8

1 tbsp olive oil

5 garlic cloves, peeled and very finely chopped

700 g/1½ lb fish cut into 5 cm/2 inch pieces

1 onion, peeled and diced

225 g/8 oz prawns (shrimp), deveined and shelled

125 g/4 oz scallops

425 g/15 oz/2 cups canned chopped tomatoes

250 ml/8 fl oz/1 cup white wine or clam juice

250 ml/8 fl oz/1 cup fish or vegetable stock

25 g/1 oz/¼ cup freshly chopped parsley, plus extra to garnish

2 tbsp lemon juice

1 tbsp tomato purée (paste)

¾ tsp salt, or to taste

½ tsp chili (red pepper) flakes

Heat the olive oil in a frying pan over a medium heat. Add the garlic and sauté until
golden. Put the garlic in the cooking dish of a 4.5–7 litre/8–12 pint/4–6 quart slow cooker.

Fry the fish in the same frying pan to add a bit of colour and to add crispness, then add
to the cooking dish with the remaining ingredients. Cover and cook on High for 2 hours
or on Low for 4 hours.

SALMON & COURGETTE RISOTTO

Creamy tender risotto without all the stirring.

Serves 2 as a main dish or 4 as a starter (appetizer)

2 tbsp olive oil

2 shallots, peeled and very finely chopped

1 courgette (zucchini), sliced

225 g/8 oz/1¼ cups Arborio rice

750 ml/1¼ pints/3 cups boiling vegetable stock

125 ml/4 fl oz/½ cup white wine or extra stock

450 g/1 lb salmon fillet, skinned, boned and diced

3 tbsp freshly chopped dill

salt and freshly ground black pepper

Put the olive oil in the cooking dish of a 4.5 litre/8 pint/4 quart slow cooker and switch to High, then stir in the shallots and courgette (zucchini). Cover and cook for 30 minutes.

Add the rice to the dish, stir, then pour in the boiling stock and wine or extra stock. Cover and cook on High for 1 hour or on Low for 2½ hours, stirring once halfway through cooking. Stir the diced salmon and dill into the risotto and season with salt and pepper. Cook for a further 15 minutes, or until the rice is tender and the salmon just cooked.

Switch off the slow cooker and leave the risotto to stand for 5 minutes.

FISH WITH HOT SALSA

Looking for a tropical escape? This dish with mango salsa brings the tropics to you.

Serves 4

8 x 175 g/6 oz white fish fillets (e.g. cod or lemon sole), skinned

150 ml/¼ pint/⅔ cup orange juice

2 tbsp lemon juice

lime wedges, if liked, to garnish

2 tbsp freshly chopped mint or spring onions (scallions)

salad leaves, to serve

FOR THE HOT SALSA

1 small mango, peeled, pitted and finely chopped

8 cherry tomatoes, quartered

1 small red onion, peeled and very finely chopped

pinch sugar

1 red chili, top cut off, slit lengthways, deseeded and very finely chopped

2 tbsp rice vinegar

zest and juice of 1 lime

1 tbsp olive oil

sea salt and freshly ground black pepper

First, make the salsa. Place the mango in a small bowl. Add the cherry tomatoes, onion, sugar and chili. Pour in the vinegar, lime zest, juice and oil. Season to taste with salt and pepper. Mix thoroughly and leave to stand for 30 minutes to allow the flavours to develop.

If the fillets are thin, like sole, lay them on a board, skinned-side up, and pile the salsa on the tail end of the fillets. Fold the fillets in half, season with salt and pepper and place in the cooking dish of a 4.5 litre/8 pint/4 quart slow cooker. If the fillets are thicker, place them directly in the dish, top with the salsa and season.

Pour the citrus juices over the fish, then place the dish in the slow cooker and cover with the lid. Switch the cooker to High and cook for 30 minutes, or Low for 1 hour.

Check that the orange and lemon juices have not evaporated. If necessary, add 3–4 tablespoons more juice or water. Switch the cooker to Low and continue to cook for 30 minutes, or until the fish is opaque and cooked through. Garnish with lime wedges, if using, and mint or spring onions (scallions), and serve immediately with salad leaves.

SALMON WITH DILL CREAM

At the fish counter, ask for a cut from the centre or top rather than the tail end so that the fillet has the same thickness throughout. This will ensure even cooking.

Serves 8

½ bunch fresh dill

1 orange, sliced

1 lemon, sliced

3 tbsp water

1.1 kg/2½ lb salmon fillet, skin on

1 tsp sea salt

½ tsp freshly ground black pepper

FOR THE DILL CREAM SAUCE

125 ml/4 fl oz/½ cup sour cream

50 g/2 oz/¼ cup mayonnaise

1 tsp grated lemon rind

1 tbsp lemon juice

½ tsp Dijon mustard

Place a piece of foil in a large, preferably oval, 7 litre/12 pint/6 quart slow cooker, long enough to hang over the sides. Coat the foil and slow cooker sides with cooking spray.

Chop enough dill fronds to equal 2 tablespoons; set aside. Line the slow cooker bottom with the remaining dill, and the orange and lemon slices. Sprinkle with the water.

Season the flesh side of the salmon with the salt and pepper and place the fillet, skin-side down, on top of the citrus. Cover and cook on Low for 2½ hours, or until the fish flakes easily when tested with a fork. Using the foil as handles, lift the fish out of the slow cooker and leave to stand for 10 minutes. Lift the fillet off the herbs and transfer to a serving platter.

While the salmon cooks, combine the reserved dill fronds, sour cream, mayonnaise, lemon rind, lemon juice and mustard in a bowl and refrigerate. Serve the salmon warm or at room temperature with the dill cream sauce.

Note:

If desired, you can cut fillets into serving sizes and place under the grill (broiler) to crisp the edges.

COCONUT THAI PRAWNS
with Rice

Zesty limes, bright peppers, grated carrots, mangetout (snow peas) and coconut tossed together with prawns (shrimp) and rice makes a satisfying dish to serve your family.

Serves 6

900 ml/1½ pints/scant 4 cups chicken stock

250 ml/8 fl oz/1 cup water or extra chicken stock

1 tsp ground coriander

1 tsp curry powder

1 tsp ground cumin

1 tsp salt

¾ tsp cayenne pepper

juice and finely cut zest of 2 limes

7 garlic cloves, peeled and very finely chopped

1 onion, peeled and diced

1 yellow, orange or red pepper, diced

1 carrot, peeled and grated

15 g/½ oz/¼ cup coconut flakes

25 g/1 oz/¼ cup sultanas (golden raisins)

350 g/12 oz/2 cups white long-grain rice

450 g/1 lb peeled deveined cooked tiger prawns (jumbo shrimp), thawed if frozen

½ cup mangetout (snow peas), cut into thin strips (optional)

TO GARNISH (OPTIONAL)

toasted coconut flakes

lemon or lime wedges

Place all the ingredients, except the prawns (shrimp) and mangetout (snow peas), in the cooking dish of a 4.5 litre/8 pint/4 quart slow cooker and stir to combine. Cover and cook on Low for 3½ hours, or until the rice is just tender.

Stir in the prawns and mangetout, if using, then cover again and cook on Low for 30 minutes.

Serve topped with toasted coconut and lemon or lime wedges, if desired. Squeeze the juice from the wedges over the rice.

GINGER & CHILI STEAMED POLLOCK

One of our favourite ways to cook fish is in a foil or baking parchment packet. It's simple and delicately steams the fish to perfection.

Serves 4

4 large (150–200 g/5–7 oz) pollock fillets
1 tbsp olive oil
2 garlic cloves, peeled and finely sliced
1 tbsp freshly grated root ginger
1 small red chili, deseeded and finely sliced
soy sauce, for sprinkling
salt and freshly ground black pepper

Lay out a large piece of foil. Place the fish side by side in the centre of the foil and drizzle oil evenly over them. Top with the garlic, ginger and chili, then sprinkle with soy sauce and season with salt and pepper.

Fold the foil over the fish to create a sealed parcel. Place the parcel in the cooking dish of a 7 litre/12 pint/6 quart slow cooker. Cover and cook on High for 2 hours or on Low for 4 hours.

Note:

Use tongs when removing the parcel from the slow cooker, as the foil will become hot.

MEAT DISHES

MADRAS LAMB

A classic hot and tangy south Indian dish with toasted spices in a rich sauce. Preparing Madras Lamb in the slow cooker helps the flavours develop and helps the lamb become meltingly tender.

Serves 4-6

450 g/1 lb lean lamb, such as fillet (tenderloin)

2 tbsp vegetable oil

1 tsp black mustard seeds

1 tbsp crushed dried chilies

1 tsp ground cumin

1 tsp ground coriander

1 tsp paprika

1 tsp ground turmeric

2–4 garlic cloves, peeled and crushed

5 cm/2 inch piece fresh root ginger, peeled and grated

1 onion, peeled and chopped

1 tbsp tomato purée (paste)

450 ml/¾ pint/1¾ cups lamb stock

TO SERVE

1 tbsp freshly chopped coriander (cilantro)

freshly cooked basmati rice

Trim the lamb and cut into small chunks. Heat the oil in a saucepan, add the mustard seeds and crushed chilies and fry for 1–2 minutes.

Add the remaining spices with the garlic and ginger and cook, stirring, for 5 minutes.

Add the meat and onion to the pan and cook, stirring, until coated in the spices.

Blend the tomato purée (paste) with the stock and pour into the pan. Bring to the boil, then carefully pour into the cooking dish of a 4.5 litre/8 pint/4 quart slow cooker. Cover and cook on Low for 5–6 hours.

Sprinkle with the chopped coriander (cilantro) and serve with freshly cooked basmati rice.

HEARTY BEEF STEW

This stew is filled with delicious beef and vegetables, and best of all, it doesn't take much work to make. Like any slow cooker recipe, this beef stew is absolutely open to all sorts of additions and adjustments. You can also brown the meat before adding to the slow cooker, if desired, for more colour and depth of flavour.

Serves 6

1 large onion, peeled and chopped

2 carrots, peeled and sliced

2 large potatoes, cut into 2.5 cm/1 inch chunks

450 g/1 lb stewing beef

750 ml/1¼ pints/3 cups beef stock

2 tbsp light brown sugar

2 tsp Worcestershire sauce

3 garlic cloves, very finely chopped

1 tsp fresh thyme

1 bay leaf

¾ tsp salt

freshly ground black pepper

1½ tbsp cornflour (cornstarch)

2 tsp tomato purée (paste)

25 g/1 oz/½ cup freshly chopped parsley or basil, for sprinkling

Put all the ingredients except the cornflour (cornstarch) and tomato purée (paste) into the cooking dish of a 4.5 litre/8 pint/4 quart slow cooker and stir to combine.

Cover and cook on High for 4–5 hours or Low for 8–9 hours until the beef is tender and the potatoes are fork-tender.

About 30 minutes before serving, mix the cornflour and tomato purée together in a small bowl. Spoon a ladleful of stock into the bowl and whisk until smooth, then stir the mixture into the stew and cook for the remaining cooking time.

Serve with a sprinkling of parsley or basil.

LAMB BALTI

Asafoetida is used in small quantities and can be found in Asian grocery shops. Quite powerfully flavoured on its own, asafoetida adds an onion-like flavour to the dish.

Serves 4–6

450 g/1 lb lean lamb, such as fillet (tenderloin), trimmed

2 tbsp vegetable oil or ghee

1 tsp mustard seeds

1 tsp ground coriander

1 tsp ground cumin

½ tsp ground turmeric

½ tsp asafoetida

1 tsp garam masala

2–3 garlic cloves, peeled and crushed

2–3 green chilies, deseeded and chopped

2 onions, peeled and chopped

350 g/12 oz sweet potatoes, peeled and cut into chunks

200 g/7 oz/1½ cups fresh or frozen green beans, trimmed

4 tomatoes, chopped

2 tsp tomato purée (paste)

600 ml/1 pint/2½ cups lamb or vegetable stock

TO SERVE

2 tbsp freshly chopped coriander (cilantro)

naan bread

Cut the lamb into chunks and set aside. Heat the oil or ghee in a large frying pan, add the mustard seeds and fry for 30 seconds, or until they pop.

Add the remaining spices and cook for 2 minutes, stirring, before adding the garlic, chilies, onions, sweet potatoes and green beans. Cook, stirring, for a further 5 minutes, or until the vegetables are coated in the spices.

Add the lamb and continue to fry for 5–8 minutes until sealed. Stir in the chopped tomatoes. Blend the tomato purée (paste) with the stock, then pour into the pan. Bring to the boil, then transfer to the cooking dish of a 4.5 litre/8 pint/4 quart slow cooker. Cover and cook on Low for 6–8 hours until the lamb is tender.

Sprinkle with chopped coriander and serve with plenty of naan bread.

LAMB MEATBALLS

Meatballs are always a family favourite, and spiced lamb meatballs with fresh coriander (cilantro) makes for a fun twist.

Serves 6

900 g/2 lb minced (ground) lamb, or half lamb and half beef

25 g/1 oz/¾ cup fresh breadcrumbs (made from day-old bread)

1 small onion, peeled and coarsely grated

20 g/¾ oz/⅔ cup freshly chopped coriander (cilantro)

2 medium (large) eggs

2 garlic cloves, peeled and very finely chopped

½ tbsp paprika

1 tsp ground cumin

½ tsp ground cinnamon

salt and freshly ground black pepper

3 tsp olive oil

FOR THE SAUCE

700 g/1½ lb/3½ cups canned whole tomatoes, crushed with hands

250 ml/8 fl oz/1 cup water

175 g/6 oz/½ cup tomato purée (paste)

2 tbsp freshly chopped basil or coriander, or to taste

1 tsp paprika

1 tsp fennel seeds

1 tsp ground cumin

¼ tsp ground cinnamon

½ tsp crushed chili (red pepper) flakes

To make the meatballs, mix together the minced (ground) lamb, breadcrumbs, onion, coriander (cilantro), eggs, garlic, spices and salt and pepper in a large bowl.

Heat the oil in a large frying pan over a medium-high heat and, when hot, brown the meatballs on all sides in batches. Transfer the browned meatballs to the cooking dish of a 7 litre/12 pint/6 quart slow cooker and continue browning the remaining meatballs.

For the sauce, mix the tomatoes, water, tomato purée (paste), basil, paprika, fennel seeds, cumin, cinnamon, chili (red pepper) flakes and salt and pepper together in a bowl and pour over the meatballs, making sure they are completely submerged.

Cover and cook on Low for 6–7 hours.

BEEF BOURGUIGNON

Long, slow cooking ensures tenderness and flavour for this version of a traditional French dish. For variety, add 450 g/1 lb mushrooms when you add the carrots.

Serves 4

700 g/1½ lb braising steak, trimmed

225 g/8 oz piece pork belly or lardons

2 tbsp olive oil

12 shallots, peeled

2 garlic cloves, peeled and sliced

225 g/8 oz carrots, peeled and sliced

2 tbsp plain (all-purpose) flour or 1 tbsp cornflour (cornstarch)

3 tbsp brandy (optional)

150 ml/¼ pint/⅔ cup red wine, such as a Burgundy

450 ml/¾ pint/1¾ cups beef stock

1 bay leaf

salt and freshly ground black pepper

450 g/1 lb small potatoes, peeled and cut into quarters

1 tbsp freshly chopped parsley, to garnish (optional)

Cut the steak and pork into small pieces and reserve.

Heat 1 tablespoon of the oil in a frying pan, add the meat and cook in batches for 5–8 minutes until seared. Remove with a slotted spoon and reserve.

Add the remaining oil to the pan, then add the shallots, garlic and carrots and cook for 10 minutes.

Return the meat to the shallots and sprinkle in the flour. Cook for 2 minutes, stirring occasionally, before pouring in the brandy, if using. Heat for 1 minute, then take off the heat and ignite.

When the flames have subsided, pour in the wine and stock. Return to the heat and bring to the boil, stirring constantly.

Transfer to the cooking dish of a 4.5–7 litre/7–12 pint/4–6 quart slow cooker. Cut the potatoes in half and stir into the meat. Add the bay leaf and season to taste with salt and pepper. Cover and cook on High for 4–5 hours or Low for 8–10 hours until the meat and potatoes are tender. Serve sprinkled with chopped parsley, if liked.

BRAISED LAMB CHOPS

Lamb chops become extremely tender in this fragrant braised dish. Serve over pasta, couscous, roasted squash, cauliflower or sweet potatoes.

Serves 4

1 tbsp vegetable oil

4 lamb loin chops or shoulder chops

2 tbsp plain (all-purpose) flour

150 ml/¼ pint/⅔ cup beef or chicken stock

425 g/15 oz/2 cups canned chopped tomatoes

1 garlic clove, peeled and very finely chopped

scant 1 tbsp tomato purée (paste)

4 celery stalks, thinly sliced

1 tsp salt

freshly ground black pepper

freshly chopped parsley

Heat the oil in a frying pan over a medium-high heat. Coat the lamb chops with flour and brown quickly in the hot oil. Transfer the chops to the cooking dish of a 4.5 litre/8 pint/4 quart slow cooker.

Bring the stock, tomatoes, garlic, tomato purée (paste), celery and salt and pepper to the boil in a pan, stirring occasionally. Pour the hot tomato mixture over the lamb in the slow cooker.

Cover and cook on High for 30 minutes, then switch to Low for 5–7 hours. Taste to check seasoning and serve sprinkled with plenty of chopped parsley.

STEAK & KIDNEY STEW

This slow-cooked stew is the ultimate winter warmer loaded with delicious dumplings.

Serves 4

1 tbsp olive oil

1 onion, peeled and chopped

2–3 garlic cloves, peeled and crushed

2 celery stalks, sliced

550 g/1 lb 3 oz diced braising steak

125 g/4 oz lambs' kidneys, cored and chopped

2 tbsp plain (all-purpose) flour

1 tbsp tomato purée (paste)

900 ml/1½ pints/scant 4 cups beef stock

salt and freshly ground black pepper

1 fresh bay leaf

300 g/11 oz carrots, peeled and sliced

350 g/12 oz new potatoes, scrubbed and quartered

FOR THE DUMPLINGS

125 g/4 oz/1 cup self-raising (self-rising) flour

50 g/2 oz/scant ½ cup shredded suet (lard)

1 tbsp freshly chopped mixed herbs

2–3 tbsp water

Heat the oil in a large, heavy-based saucepan, add the onion, garlic and celery and sauté for 5 minutes, or until browned. Remove and reserve. Add the steak and kidneys to the pan and cook for 3–5 minutes until sealed, then return the onion mixture to the pan.

Sprinkle in the flour and cook, stirring, for 2 minutes. Take off the heat, stir in the tomato purée (paste), then the stock, and season to taste with salt and pepper. Add the bay leaf.

Return to the heat and bring to the boil, stirring occasionally. Add the carrots and potatoes, then carefully transfer to the cooking dish of a 4.5 litre/8 pint/4 quart slow cooker. Cover and cook on High for 1 hour, then switch to Low and cook for 6–8 hours.

Place the flour, suet (lard) and herbs in a bowl and add salt and pepper to taste. Add the water and mix to a stiff mixture. Using a little extra flour as needed, shape into 8 small balls. Place the dumplings on top of the stew and cover with the lid. Return the slow cooker to High and cook for 30–60 minutes before serving.

JAMBALAYA

Featuring chicken, prawns (shrimp) and smoked sausage, this classic Creole rice dish is perfect for the slow cooker, as all the flavours blend together wonderfully over time.

Serves 8

900 g/2 lb skinless, boneless chicken thighs

450 g/1 lb smoked sausage, cut into 5 cm/2 inch slices

1 large onion, peeled and chopped

1 large green pepper, deseeded and chopped

3 celery stalks, chopped

700 g/1½ lb/3½ cups canned chopped tomatoes with juice

3 garlic cloves, peeled and chopped

500 ml/18 fl oz/2 cups chicken stock

1 tbsp Cajun or Creole spice mix

1 tsp dried thyme

1 tsp dried oregano

1 lb extra large prawns (shrimp), peeled and deveined

325 g/11½ oz/1¾ cups long-grain rice

freshly chopped parsley (optional)

Combine the chicken, sausage, onion, green pepper, celery, tomatoes, garlic, stock, spice mix, thyme and oregano in a 6 litre/10½ pint/5 quart slow cooker. Cover and cook on Low for 5 hours.

Add the prawns (shrimp) and rice, increase the heat to High and cook for a further 30 minutes until the rice is tender. Sprinkle with chopped parsley, if desired.

MASSAMAN BEEF CURRY

Slow-cooked, meltingly tender beef and a sprinkling of crunchy peanuts to finish – it's curry heaven in a bowl!

Serves 4–6

450 g/1 lb braising steak

2 tbsp vegetable oil

5 cm/2 inch piece fresh root ginger, peeled and grated

3 green bird's-eye chilies, deseeded and chopped

2 red onions, peeled and chopped

3 garlic cloves, peeled and crushed

2 tbsp Massaman Thai curry paste

400 ml/14 fl oz/1⅔ cups canned coconut milk

150–200 ml/5–7 fl oz/⅔–¾ cup beef stock

350 g/12 oz new potatoes, scrubbed and cut into chunks

1 green pepper, deseeded and cut into strips (optional)

65 g/2½ oz/½ cup roasted peanuts

Trim the beef, cut into thin strips and reserve. Heat the oil in a heavy-based frying pan, add the ginger and chilies and fry for 3 minutes. Add the onions and garlic and continue to fry for 5 minutes, or until the onions have softened.

Remove the onions and garlic with a slotted spoon and add the beef to the pan. Cook, stirring, for 5 minutes, or until sealed.

Add the curry paste and continue to fry for 3 minutes, then return the onions and garlic to the pan and stir well.

Pour the coconut milk and stock into the pan and add the new potatoes, then bring to the boil. Transfer to the cooking dish of a 4.5 litre/8 pint/4 quart slow cooker and cover with the lid. Switch to auto and cook for 2 hours.

Add the green pepper to the meat, if using, and switch the slow cooker to Low. Cook for 6–8 hours until the meat and potatoes are done. Sprinkle the peanuts over the curry and serve.

IRISH BEEF & GUINNESS STEW

The maltiness of dark beer really does amazing things for this gravy, giving it a deep, complex, rich flavour. Serve with some crusty country bread or Irish soda bread. This stew is even better the next day.

Serves 8

900 g/2 lb beef chuck

1½ tsp salt, or to taste

¼ tsp freshly ground black pepper, or to taste

3 tbsp plain (all-purpose) flour or 1½ tbsp cornflour (cornstarch)

175 g/6 oz bacon rashers (slices), diced

2 medium-large onions, peeled and chopped

600 ml/1 pint/2½ cups Guinness Extra Stout

3 garlic cloves, peeled and very finely chopped

4 medium firm, waxy potatoes, cut into 2.5 cm/1 inch pieces

2 large carrots, peeled and chopped into 1 cm/½ inch pieces

2 celery stalks, chopped into ½ inch pieces

1 large parsnip, peeled and chopped into 1 cm/½ inch pieces

250 ml/8 fl oz/1 cup beef stock

2 tbsp Worcestershire sauce

1 tbsp tomato purée (paste)

1 tsp dried thyme

1 tsp dried rosemary

2 bay leaves

Cut the beef across the grain into 2.5 cm/1 inch pieces. Sprinkle with the salt, pepper and flour and toss to coat the pieces. Reserve.

Fry the bacon in a casserole dish or heavy pan until cooked, then remove it with a slotted spoon and put in the cooking dish of a 7 litre/12 pint/6 quart slow cooker, leaving the bacon fat (drippings) in the pan.

Working in batches and being careful not to overcrowd the pieces, brown the beef well on all sides. Transfer the browned beef to the cooking dish and repeat until all the beef is browned.

Add the onions to the casserole dish and fry them for 10 minutes, adding more oil if necessary, until lightly browned. Add the Guinness and bring to a rapid boil, deglazing the bottom of the dish, scraping up the browned bits on the bottom. Boil for 2 minutes.

Add the onion mixture and remaining ingredients to the cooking dish, then cover and cook on High for 3–4 hours or on Low for 6–8 hours.

KERALA PORK CURRY

Kerala-style pork curry is a little spicy and cooked in a rich, thick gravy. The flavours intensify and penetrate the meat after simmering in the slow cooker.

Serves 4-6

2 tbsp vegetable oil or ghee

1 tbsp desiccated (dry unsweetened) coconut

1 tsp mustard seeds

1 tsp fennel seeds

1 cinnamon stick, bruised

1 tsp ground cumin

1 tsp ground coriander

450 g/1 lb pork loin or fillet, trimmed and cut into small chunks or strips

1–2 red chilies, deseeded and chopped

2–3 garlic cloves, peeled and chopped

2 onions, peeled and chopped

½ tsp saffron strands

300 ml/½ pint/1¼ cups coconut milk

150 ml/¼ pint/⅔ cup water

125 g/4 oz/¾ cup frozen peas, thawed

freshly cooked basmati rice, to serve

Heat 1 teaspoon of the oil or ghee in a frying pan, add the desiccated (dry unsweetened) coconut and fry for 30 seconds, stirring, until lightly toasted. Reserve.

Add the remaining oil or ghee to the pan, add the seeds and fry for 30 seconds, or until they pop. Add the remaining spices and cook, stirring, for 2 minutes. Add the pork and fry for 5 minutes, or until sealed.

Add the chilies, garlic and onions and continue to fry for 3 minutes before stirring in the saffron strands. Stir, then pour in the coconut milk and water.

Transfer to the cooking dish of a 4.5 litre/8 pint/4 quart slow cooker and cover with the lid. Switch the slow cooker to auto and cook for 1 hour before switching the cooker to Low and cooking for 5–7 hours. Stir the peas into the cooking dish for the last 1 hour of cooking time.

Serve with freshly cooked basmati rice.

PULLED PORK TACO FILLING

For an easy Mexican meal, set and forget seasoned pork shoulder for this slow-cooked pork taco filling. These easy tacos get their fantastic flavour from a cumin, orange and lime juice and fresh jalapeño chili.

Serves 10

FOR THE RUB

    1 tbsp dried oregano

    1½ tsp salt

    2 tsp ground cumin

    1 tsp ground black pepper

    1 tbsp olive oil

FOR THE PORK

    2.5 kg/5 lb pork shoulder (pork butt), skinless, bone in or 2 kg/4 lb without bone

    1 onion, peeled and chopped

    1 jalapeño chili, deseeded and chopped

    4 garlic cloves, very finely chopped

    juice of 1 orange

    juice of 1 lime

Combine all the rub ingredients, then spread all over the pork. Place the pork in the cooking dish of a 7 litre/12 pint/6 quart slow cooker, fatty side (fat cap) up. Top with the onion, jalapeño chili and garlic and pour over the orange and lime juices.

Cover and cook on High for 6 hours or on Low for 8–10 hours. The meat should be tender and falling off the bone. Remove from the slow cooker and shred the pork using two forks.

Skim off the fat from the juices remaining in the slow cooker and discard the fat. If you are left with more than 350–500 ml/12–18 fl oz/1½–2 cups juice, then reduce it either in the slow cooker on the sauté setting with the lid off, or in a saucepan.

Pour the juices over the shredded pork. Serve with your favourite taco toppings, such as diced tomato, guacamole, shredded lettuce and/or sliced black olives.

PANCETTA & HAM RISOTTO

Creamy risotto without the stirring! It's a wonderfully easy way to make this classic Italian dish with little effort.

Serves 6

125 g/4 oz pancetta, cut into 5 mm/¼ inch cubes

200 g/7 oz smoked cured ham, cut into 5 mm/¼ inch cubes

1 litre/1¾ pints/4 cups chicken stock

225 g/8 oz/1¼ cups Arborio rice

1 tsp garlic powder

½ tsp onion powder

10 fresh sage leaves, chopped, or ½ tbsp dried sage

1 tsp salt, or to taste

¼ tsp ground black pepper

20 g/¾ oz/⅔ cup grated Parmesan cheese

Cook the pancetta in a small nonstick pan over a medium heat for 5 minutes, stirring constantly, until crispy.

Mix the pancetta, ham, stock, rice, garlic powder, onion powder, sage and salt and pepper in the dish of a 4.5 litre/8 pint/4 quart slow cooker. Stir well. Cover and cook on High for 2 hours or on Low for 4 hours until the rice is tender, stirring twice during cooking.

Stir in the Parmesan cheese. Cover and cook for about 10 minutes until the cheese is melted.

SLOW-BRAISED BBQ RIBS

Tender, slow-braised ribs get their final caramelization from the grill (broiler). Leave the rub on the ribs overnight to achieve the best flavour.

Serves 6

FOR THE SAUCE

450 g/1 lb/2 cups tomato ketchup

250 ml/8 fl oz/1 cup water

50 ml/2 fl oz/¼ cup cider vinegar

8 tbsp brown sugar

½ tbsp ground black pepper

½ tbsp dry mustard

½–1 tsp crushed chili (red pepper) flakes

1 tsp garlic powder

1 tsp onion powder

1 tsp paprika

1 tbsp molasses

½ tbsp lemon juice

½ tbsp Worcestershire sauce

pinch cayenne pepper (optional)

salt, to taste

FOR THE RIBS

2 slabs of ribs, about 3–4 kg/6–8 lb

1 tbsp dry mustard

1 tbsp black pepper

1 tbsp onion powder

1 tbsp garlic powder

1 tbsp paprika

1 tbsp soft brown sugar

½ tbsp salt

2 tbsp extra virgin olive oil

For the sauce, mix all the ingredients together well in a medium pan. Bring to the boil, reduce the heat and simmer for about 15 minutes, stirring occasionally. Cool, then refrigerate until ready to use.

Rinse the ribs and pat dry. Flip the ribs over and remove the membrane (the thin white film) that is on the back side of the ribs, and discard.

For the rub, mix the dry mustard, pepper, onion powder, garlic powder, paprika, brown sugar and salt together in a bowl. Coat the ribs with olive oil on both sides and rub in the seasoning blend on both sides. Cover the ribs and marinate in the refrigerator overnight.

When ready to cook in the slow cooker, remove the ribs from the refrigerator and place them into the cooking dish of a 7 litre/12 pint/6 quart slow cooker, cutting as needed to fit. Spoon half of the barbecue sauce between the layers of ribs. Cover and cook on Low for 6–7 hours until the ribs are tender and cooked through.

Preheat the grill (broiler). Place the ribs on a rimmed baking sheet, discarding the juices. Baste the ribs with the remaining barbecue sauce and grill (broil) for about 5–7 minutes until a nice crust forms on top of the ribs. Slice the ribs and serve.

CHILI CON CARNE

Chili con carne is an all-round crowd pleaser. Cooking it in a slow cooker allows all the flavours to really develop.

Serves 8–10

2 tbsp olive oil

1 onion, peeled and chopped

4 garlic cloves, peeled and finely chopped

1 green pepper

1.3 kg/3 lb minced (ground) beef

2 tbsp olive oil

4–6 tbsp chili powder, or to taste

1 tbsp ground cumin

1 tbsp dried oregano

1 tbsp hot pepper sauce

1 tsp cayenne pepper

3 tbsp masa harina or coarsely ground polenta (cornmeal)

750 ml/1¼ pints/3 cups tomato juice

500 ml/18 fl oz/2 cups beef stock

425 g/15 oz/2⅔ cups canned kidney beans, drained and rinsed

salt and freshly ground black pepper

Heat the oil in a pan, add the onion, garlic and green pepper and fry until soft. Add the minced (ground) beef and fry until lightly browned. Put into the cooking dish of a 4.5 litre/8 pint/4 quart slow cooker.

Blend the chili powder, cumin, oregano, pepper sauce, cayenne pepper and masa harina together in a bowl. Stir into the meat, then add the tomato juice and stock.

Cover and cook on High for 3½ hours or on Low for 7 hours. One hour before serving, add the kidney beans.

Check the seasoning, adding more salt and pepper if needed before serving.

LAMB TAGINE

Braising an inexpensive cut like lamb shoulder in the Moroccan way transforms the meat into a thick, aromatic stew of meltingly tender meat, chickpeas and dried fruit. If you like, steam the couscous with a large pinch of saffron.

Serves 6-8

125 g/4 oz/¾ cup dried chickpeas

2 tbsp olive oil

1.3 kg/3 lb lamb shoulder, cut into 2.5 cm/1 inch cubes

sea salt and freshly ground black pepper

5 garlic cloves, 2 whole and 3 very finely chopped

1 large cinnamon stick, broken in half

1 large onion, diced

5 tsp Ras-el-Hanout spice blend (*see* note)

1 tbsp freshly chopped root ginger

200 g/7 oz/1 cup canned diced tomatoes with juice

about 600 ml/1 pint/2½ cups low-salt chicken stock

65 g/2½ oz/½ cup halved dried apricots

TO SERVE

steamed couscous

freshly chopped coriander (cilantro)

Place the chickpeas in a medium saucepan and pour in enough water to cover by 5 cm/2 inches. Soak overnight.

The next day, drain the chickpeas, rinse and put in the cooking dish of a 4.5–6 litre/8–12 pint/4–6 quart slow cooker.

Heat the oil in a large, heavy frying pan over a medium-high heat. Season the lamb with salt and pepper, then, working in batches, brown the lamb on all sides, about 4 minutes per batch. Transfer the lamb to the cooking dish. Add the whole garlic cloves and cinnamon.

In the same frying pan, add the onion, seasoning and ginger and stir-fry for 2 minutes, or until the onion is soft. Transfer to the slow cooker and add all the remaining ingredients. Cover and cook on High for 4 hours or Low for 8 hours.

Serve with couscous and sprinkle with coriander (cilantro).

Note:

To make your own Ras-el-Hanout, mix together ¾ teaspoons each ground cumin, ground ginger and salt, ½ teaspoon each ground black pepper, ground cinnamon, ground coriander seeds, cayenne pepper and ground allspice, and ¼ teaspoon ground cloves.

CASSOULET

This is an easy version of cassoulet, filled to the brim with white beans, crisp bacon, pork and chorizo sausage.

Serves 10

1.8 kg/4 lb boneless pork shoulder, cut into 8 pieces and trimmed of excess fat
salt and freshly ground pepper
125 g/4 oz thick-cut bacon rashers (slices), cut crossways into 1 cm/½ inch strips
700 g/1½ lb fresh chorizo sausage, cut into diagonal chunks
3 onions, peeled and roughly chopped
500 ml/18 fl oz/2 cups dry white wine, such as Sauvignon Blanc
1 tbsp tomato purée (paste)
900 g/2 lb/4⅓ cups canned Italian plum tomatoes, peeled, drained and roughly chopped
500 ml/18 fl oz/2 cups chicken stock
2 kg/4½ lb/12 cups dried cannellini, haricot or Great Northern beans, or other small
   white beans, soaked overnight, then cooked and drained
1 garlic head, cloves peeled and chopped
25 g/1 oz/¼ cup chopped fresh flat-leaf parsley, plus extra to garnish

Season the pork generously with salt and pepper and set aside.

Heat a frying pan over a medium-high heat. Add the bacon and cook for 5 minutes, or until crisp on both sides. Drain on paper towels. Reserve the bacon fat in the pan.

Add half of the pork to the pan and brown on all sides for 7–8 minutes total. Transfer to the cooking dish of a 7 litre/12 pint/6 quart slow cooker and repeat with the remaining pork. Brown the chorizo sausage as well.

Add the onions and ½ teaspoon salt to the frying pan and cook for 7 minutes, stirring occasionally, until golden brown and softened. Add the wine and simmer until reduced by half, about 8 minutes. Stir in the tomato purée (paste), tomatoes and stock and stir to deglaze the pan. Pour the mixture into the cooking dish of the slow cooker.

Add the beans and garlic. Cover and cook on Low for 9–10 hours until the pork pulls apart easily. Fold in the parsley. Adjust the seasonings with salt and pepper, as needed.

POULTRY

CALYPSO CHICKEN

A delicious meal perfumed with the enchanting flavours of the Caribbean – allspice and coconut.

Serves 4–6

2 onions

2 tbsp groundnut (peanut) oil

450 g/1 lb skinless, boneless chicken breast, chopped

3 garlic cloves, peeled and sliced

1–2 chilies, deseeded and sliced

1 tsp ground coriander

1 tsp ground cumin

1 tsp ground turmeric

1 tsp ground allspice

600 ml/1 pint/2½ cups chicken stock

200 g/7 oz/1¼ cups canned red kidney beans, drained and rinsed

1 large red pepper, deseeded and diced

½ whole pineapple, cut into chunks

15 g/½ oz toasted unsweetened coconut chips or 1 tbsp freshly chopped coriander (cilantro), to garnish

freshly cooked rice, to serve

Peel the onions and, keeping the root intact, slcie into thin wedges. Heat the oil in a heavy-based saucepan, add the chicken and brown on all sides. Remove from the pan and place in the cooking dish of a 4.5 litre/8 pint/4 quart slow cooker.

Add the onions, garlic and chilies to the pan and fry for 5–8 minutes until lightly browned. Sprinkle in all the spices and cook, stirring, for 2 minutes.

Add the stock to the pan and bring to the boil, then carefully transfer to the cooking dish. Add the beans, cover and cook on High for 3 hours. Stir in the pepper and pineapple and continue to cook for 45–60 minutes, or until the chicken is thoroughly cooked.

Spoon into a warmed serving dish, sprinkle with toasted coconut or chopped coriander (cilantro) and serve with rice.

KUNG PAO CHICKEN

To make this dish, start by coating the chicken in cornflour (cornstarch) and browning it before adding it into the slow cooker. It's an extra step, but it makes a big difference in colour and flavour.

Serves 6

FOR THE CHICKEN

450 g/1 lb skinless, boneless chicken breast/thighs, cut into bite-size pieces

75 g/3 oz/⅔ cup cornflour (cornstarch)

¼ tsp ground black pepper

1 tbsp groundnut (peanut) or olive oil

FOR THE SAUCE (DOUBLE IF EXTRA SAUCE DESIRED)

125 ml/4 fl oz/½ cup soy sauce

100 ml/3½ fl oz/⅓ cup water

3 tbsp honey

3 tbsp hoisin sauce

3 garlic cloves, peeled and very finely chopped

1 tsp freshly grated root ginger

¼–½ tsp chili (red pepper) flakes

FOR THE VEGETABLES

2 tbsp cornflour (cornstarch)

3 tbsp water

450 g/1 lb pak choi (bok choy) or baby bok choy, chopped

100 g/3½ oz/1 cup mung beansprouts

4–6 dried red chilies, to taste, or ½–1 tsp chili (red pepper) flakes (optional)

75 g/3 oz/⅔ cup roasted peanuts or cashews

TO SERVE

2 salad (green) onions, thinly sliced

freshly cooked rice

Toss the chicken, cornflour (cornstarch) and black pepper together in a bowl until the chicken is coated evenly.

Heat the oil in a frying pan over a medium-high heat and cook the chicken for 2–3 minutes until lightly browned. Transfer to the cooking dish of a 4.5–7 litre/8–12 pint/4–6 quart slow cooker.

For the sauce, whisk the soy sauce, water, honey, hoisin sauce, garlic, ginger and chili (red pepper) flakes together in a bowl, then pour over the chicken.

Cover and cook on High for 1½–2½ hours or on Low for 3–5 hours.

About 30 minutes before serving, whisk the cornflour (cornstarch) and water together in a small bowl and stir into the slow cooker dish. Add the pak choi (bok choy), beansprouts, dried chilies or chili (pepper) flakes, if using, and peanuts. Cover and cook on High for a further 30 minutes, or until the vegetables are tender and the sauce is thick.

Sprinkle with salad (green) onions and serve with rice.

CHICKEN GUMBO

Slow cooking helps the seasonings really incorporate into the dish, creating tender chicken and vegetables that are simply full of flavour.

Serves 4

8 small skinless chicken thighs

1 tbsp olive oil

15 g/½ oz/1 tbsp unsalted butter

1 onion, peeled and chopped

2–3 garlic cloves, peeled and chopped

1–2 red chilies, deseeded and chopped

2 celery stalks, sliced

1 red pepper, deseeded and chopped

225 g/8 oz okra, trimmed and sliced

4 spicy sausages

2 tbsp plain (all-purpose) flour or 1 tbsp cornflour (cornstarch)

1.7 litres/3 pints/7 cups chicken stock

few dashes Tabasco sauce

cooked rice, to serve

Rinse the chicken thighs or breasts and pat dry. Heat the oil and butter in a large, heavy-based saucepan, add the chicken and fry, in batches, for 8–10 minutes until lightly browned. Remove with a slotted spoon or metal tongs and put in the cooking dish of a 4.5–7 litre/8–12 pint/4–6 quart slow cooker.

Add all the vegetables to the pan and fry for 8 minutes, or until the vegetables are beginning to soften. Remove with a slotted spoon and reserve half of the vegetable mixture in a covered container in the refrigerator. Reserve the second half of the vegetables.

Add the sausages to the pan and cook for 5–8 minutes until browned all over, then remove and cut each sausage in half. Place the sausages into the cooking dish.

Add the reserved half of the browned vegetables to the pan and sprinkle in the flour. Cook for 2 minutes, then gradually stir in the stock. Bring to the boil, then pour into the cooking dish over the chicken and sausages. Cover and cook on High for 3 hours or Low for 6 hours.

If liked, remove the chicken and shred with a fork, before returning to the dish. Add the remaining chilled vegetables together with a few dashes of Tabasco. Cover again and cook on High for 30 minutes. Serve with rice.

CHICKEN TAMALES

Make forming the tamales a family activity by setting up a task for everyone: one person placing the filling on the corn husks, another folding and a third tying.

Serves 8-10

FOR THE CORN HUSKS

24 dried corn husks

FOR THE SAUCE

1 litre/1¾ pints/4 cups chicken stock

3 dried ancho chilies, deseeded

1 tbsp olive oil

1½ onions, peeled and chopped

2 tsp dried oregano

2 tsp salt

8 garlic cloves, peeled and finely chopped

2 chipotle chilies, canned in adobo sauce, deseeded and very finely chopped

2 tbsp unsalted tomato purée (paste)

1½ tsp ground cumin

425 g/15 oz canned unsalted tomato sauce

25 g/1 oz dark (semisweet) chocolate

FOR THE TAMALES

550 g/1 lb 3 oz/4 cups shredded skinless cooked chicken breast

450 g/1 lb/4 cups instant masa harina or coarsely ground polenta (cornmeal)

1½ tsp baking powder

125 g/4 oz/½ cup lard

600 ml/1 pint/2½ cups water

Submerge the corn husks in a large pot filled with warm water and soak for 30 minutes until pliable. Drain and discard the water. For the sauce, combine the stock and chilies in a saucepan. Bring to the boil, then reduce the heat and simmer for 5 minutes. Remove from the heat and leave for 5 minutes. Drain the chilies over a bowl, reserving the stock.

Heat the oil in a frying pan over a medium-high heat, add the onions and cook for 2 minutes, stirring occasionally. Reduce the heat to medium and stir in the oregano, 1 teaspoon salt and the garlic and sauté for 5 minutes. Add the chipotle and cook for 1 minute. Stir in half the reserved spiced chicken stock, the tomato purée (paste), cumin and tomato sauce and cook for 5 minutes, or until the mixture thickens slightly.

Using a hand-held stick (immersion) blender, or by working in batches in a blender, blend the ancho chili mixture until smooth. Return the mixture to a frying pan over a medium heat and stir in the chocolate. Cook for 1 minute, then remove 350 ml/12 fl oz/1½ cups of the sauce, cover and chill. Add the shredded chicken to the pan and mix into the sauce. Remove from the heat and cool to room temperature.

Combine the masa harina, baking powder and the remaining salt in a bowl. Cut in the lard with a pastry blender or 2 knives until the mixture resembles coarse meal. Add the remaining spiced chicken stock and 350 ml/12 fl oz/1½ cups water and stir until a soft dough forms. Knead the dough in the bowl until it is smooth and pliable.

To make the tamales, tear a thin strip off each corn husk. Place 1 corn husk on a work surface with the narrow end facing you. Place about 3 heaped tablespoons of the masa dough in the centre of the husk, about 2.5 cm/1 inch from the top and press into a 10 x 9 cm/4 x 3½ inch rectangle. Spoon 2½ tablespoons chicken mixture down the centre of the dough rectangle. Fold the sides of the husk over the filling, then fold the narrow end up to close the parcel at one end. Tie a husk strip around the tamale to secure and repeat with the remaining husks, dough, filling and husk strips.

Poke holes in the bottom of a 34 x 24 cm/13½ x 9½-inch shallow disposable foil pan; cut the corners from the rim down to the bottom to make it flexible. Fit the pan into the bottom of the cooking dish of a 7 litre/12 pint/6 quart oval or rectangular slow cooker, pour in the remaining water, then line the bottom of the pan with damp paper towels. Stand the tamales in the prepared pan with the open ends facing upright. Cover and cook on High for 4 hours, or until set. Let the tamales stand for 10 minutes. Heat the reserved sauce and serve with the tamales.

CHICKEN & PAPAYA CURRY

Using your slow cooker is a surprisingly easy way of making your favourite takeaway dishes in a healthier way, with less hands-on time than it takes to go and collect one!

Serves 4-6

2 tbsp groundnut (peanut) oil

450 g/1 lb skinless, boneless chicken, diced

2 red onions, peeled and cut into wedges

4 garlic cloves, peeled and sliced

5 cm/2 inch piece fresh root ginger, peeled and grated

2 tsp chili powder

1 tsp ground allspice

1 tbsp mild curry paste

1–2 limes (preferably organic)

few curry leaves

300 ml/½ pint/1¼ cups chicken stock

300 g/11 oz carrots, peeled and sliced

1 large papaya, ripe but still firm

1 green pepper, deseeded and chopped

2 small bananas, sliced

TO SERVE

freshly cooked rice and peas

Heat the oil in a heavy-based saucepan, add the chicken and brown on all sides. Remove and reserve. Add the onions, garlic and ginger to the pan and fry for 5 minutes. Add the spices and curry paste and cook for 5 minutes, stirring. Return the chicken to the pan and stir until the chicken is coated in the spices.

Finely grate 1 tablespoon of zest from the lime(s) and squeeze out 3 tablespoons of juice. Stir in the curry leaves, lime zest and juice and the stock. Add the carrots and bring to the boil. Carefully transfer to the cooking dish of a 4.5 litre/8 pint/4 quart slow cooker, cover and cook on High for 3½ hours.

Peel the papaya, then remove the seeds and chop the flesh. Add the papaya flesh to the cooking dish with the green pepper and bananas and cook for a further 30 minutes, or until the chicken is cooked. Spoon into a warmed serving dish and serve with rice and peas.

TERIYAKI CHICKEN

All of the delicious sweet and savoury teriyaki flavours you love, made with an easy homemade teriyaki sauce naturally sweetened with honey.

Serves 6

½ onion, peeled and chopped

900 g/2 lb skinless, boneless chicken breasts or thighs

175 g/6 oz/½ cup honey

125 ml/4 fl oz/½ cup soy sauce

50 ml/2 fl oz/¼ cup rice wine vinegar

1 tbsp freshly grated root ginger

2 garlic cloves, peeled and very finely chopped

⅛ tsp freshly ground black pepper

50 ml/2 fl oz/¼ cup cold water

3 tbsp cornflour (cornstarch)

freshly cooked rice, to serve

TO GARNISH

thinly sliced salad (green) onions

sesame seeds

Place the onion in the bottom of the cooking dish of a 4.5 litre/8 pint/4 quart slow cooker and top with the chicken.

Whisk the honey, soy sauce, rice wine vinegar, ginger, garlic and black pepper together in a bowl until combined, then pour the mixture on top of the chicken.

Cover and cook on High for 3½–4 hours or on Low for 7–8 hours until the chicken is cooked through and shreds easily with a fork. Remove the chicken with a slotted spoon to a separate bowl.

Whisk the cold water and cornflour (cornstarch) together in another bowl. Pour the cornflour mixture into the teriyaki sauce mixture in the cooking dish and whisk to combine. Cover and switch the slow cooker to High until the mixture has thickened, about 20–30 minutes.

Meanwhile, break the chicken into bite-size chunks using 2 forks, then stir the chicken back into the thickened sauce and heat through on High.

When the chicken is heated through and coated with the sauce, serve topped with salad (green) onions and sesame seeds over rice.

CHICKEN CHASSEUR

This French classic dish combines mushrooms and chicken in a tomato and white wine sauce. The name, literally 'hunter's chicken', refers to the natural autumn combination of game birds and mushrooms from the woods.

Serves 4

1 whole chicken, about 1.4 kg/3 lb in weight, jointed into 4 or 8 portions

1 tbsp olive oil

15 g/½ oz unsalted butter, coconut oil, or olive oil

12 baby (pearl) onions, peeled

2–4 garlic cloves, peeled and sliced

2 celery stalks, sliced

175 g/6 oz closed-cup mushrooms

2 tbsp plain (all-purpose) flour or 2 tbsp cornflour (cornstarch)

300 ml/½ pint/1¼ cups dry white wine

2 tbsp tomato purée (paste)

450 ml/¾ pint/1¾ cups chicken stock

salt and freshly ground black pepper

1 tsp dried tarragon or few fresh tarragon sprigs

300 g/11 oz/2 cups shelled fresh or frozen broad (fava) beans (optional)

16 cherry tomatoes

1 tbsp freshly chopped tarragon, to garnish

Skin the chicken, if preferred, and rinse lightly. Pat dry on absorbent paper towels.

Heat the oil and butter in a heavy-based frying pan, add the chicken portions and fry for 5–8 minutes, in batches, until browned all over. Remove with a slotted spoon and place in the cooking dish of a 4.5 litre/8 pint/4 quart slow cooker.

Add the onions, garlic and celery to the frying pan and cook for 5 minutes, or until golden. Cut the mushrooms in half if large, then add to the pan and cook for 2 minutes. Sprinkle in the flour and cook for 2 minutes, then gradually stir in the wine. Blend the tomato purée (paste) with a little of the stock in a small bowl, then stir into the pan together with the remaining stock, seasoning to taste, and the dried or fresh tarragon.

Bring to the boil, stirring constantly. Pour the sauce over the chicken, cover and cook on High for 3½ hours or on Low for 6 hours.

Add the broad (fava) beans, if using, and the cherry tomatoes, cover again and cook for a further 30 minutes, or until the chicken and vegetables are cooked. Serve sprinkled with freshly chopped tarragon.

CHICKEN PARMESAN

This is an updated take on Chicken Parmesan, which is perfect for a weeknight dinner. When you're ready to eat, just cook the pasta and dinner is served!

Serves 4

1 medium (large) egg

25 g/1 oz/⅓ cup dry breadcrumbs

40 g/1½ oz/⅓ cup grated Parmesan cheese

½ tsp Italian seasoning

¼ tsp salt

¼ tsp ground black pepper

4 skinless, boneless chicken breasts, about 575 g/1¼ lb

750 ml/1¼ pints/3¼ cups ready-made tomato pasta sauce or marinara sauce

50 g/2 oz/½ cup grated mozzarella cheese

freshly cooked pasta, to serve

Oil the cooking dish of a 2.2–3.4 litre/4–6 pint/2–3-quart slow cooker.

Beat the egg in a shallow bowl until foamy. In a separate shallow bowl, mix the breadcrumbs, Parmesan cheese, Italian seasoning and salt and pepper. Dip the chicken into the egg, then coat evenly with the breadcrumb mixture. Place the coated chicken in the cooking dish. Pour the pasta sauce evenly over the chicken. Cover and cook on Low for 5–6 hours.

Sprinkle the mozzarella over the top of the chicken. Cover and cook on Low for a further 15 minutes.

Serve the chicken over pasta.

BENGALI CHICKEN CURRY

This saucy slow-cooker Bengali chicken curry has a spicy kick! Simple ingredients bring lots of flavour to this easy-to-make family hit.

Serves 4

2–3 red chilies, deseeded and chopped, or to taste

3 garlic cloves, peeled and chopped

5 cm/2 inch piece fresh root ginger, peeled and grated

4 shallots, peeled and chopped

1 tsp ground turmeric

250 ml/8 fl oz/1 cup water

450 g/1 lb skinless chicken, boneless if preferred

2 tbsp vegetable oil, ghee or coconut oil

few curry leaves

1 tbsp freshly chopped coriander (cilantro), to garnish

TO SERVE

Indian-style bread

salad

Place the chilies, garlic, ginger, shallots, turmeric and 150 ml/¼ pint/⅔ cup of the water in a food processor until smooth, then pour into a shallow dish.

Lightly rinse the chicken and pat dry with absorbent paper towels. Cut into strips if liked, then add the chicken to the spice mixture. Cover and leave to marinate in the refrigerator for 15–30 minutes, stirring occasionally, or longer if time permits.

Heat the oil or ghee in a heavy-based frying pan, then, using a slotted spoon, remove the chicken from the marinade, reserving the marinade. Cook the chicken for 5 minutes, or until lightly browned.

Place the chicken in the cooking dish of a 4.5 litre/8 pint/4 quart slow cooker. Pour the reserved marinade over the chicken and add the curry leaves and remaining water. Cover and cook on High for 3 hours or on Low for 6 hours until the chicken is cooked through.

Spoon into a warmed serving dish, sprinkle with the chopped coriander (cilantro) and serve with bread and salad.

CHICKEN & CHICKPEA KORMA

This curry has a wonderful depth of flavour and great texture contrast from the mix of soft onions, tender chicken meat and buttery chickpeas.

Serves 4–6

350 g/12 oz skinless, boneless chicken

2 tbsp vegetable oil

2 onions, peeled and cut into wedges

2–4 garlic cloves, peeled and chopped

2–3 tbsp Korma curry paste

1 tsp garam masala

½–1 tsp ground cloves

450 ml/¾ pint/1¾ cups chicken stock

400 g/14 oz/1½ cups canned chickpeas, drained and rinsed

4 tbsp double (heavy) cream or coconut milk

1 tbsp freshly chopped coriander (cilantro), to garnish

Indian-style bread, to serve

Cut the chicken into small chunks. Heat the oil in a frying pan over a medium-high heat, add the chicken and cook, stirring, for 3 minutes, or until seared. Remove and place in the cooking dish of a 4.5 litre/8 pint/4 quart slow cooker.

Add the onions and garlic to the frying pan and cook over a medium heat for 5 minutes, or until the onions have begun to soften. Add the curry paste, garam masala and ground cloves and cook, stirring, for 2 minutes. Pour the sauce over the chicken and stir. Stir the stock and chickpeas into the chicken and onion mixture. Cover and cook on High for 3 hours, or on Low for 6 hours, or until the chicken is thoroughly cooked. Stir in the cream. Spoon into a warmed serving dish, sprinkle with the coriander (cilantro) and serve with Indian-style bread.

BUTTER CHICKEN

This is a slow-cooker Butter Chicken with all the creamy deep flavours you expect from your favourite, made in the comfort of your home.

Serves 4-6

400 ml/14 fl oz/1⅔ cups canned coconut milk

175 g/6 oz/1⅓ cups canned tomato purée (paste)

2 tbsp garam masala

1 tbsp freshly grated root ginger

3 garlic cloves, peeled and very finely chopped

2 tsp curry powder

1–2 tsp Thai red curry paste, or to taste

1 tsp cayenne pepper, or to taste

½–1 tsp ground turmeric

¼ tsp salt

½ onion, peeled and very finely chopped

450 g/1 lb skinless, boneless chicken thighs or breast, cut
   into bite-size chunks

2 tbsp butter, cold, cut into pieces

125 ml/4 fl oz/½ cup Greek yogurt

50 ml/2 fl oz/¼ cup single cream (half and half) or
   double (heavy) cream

salt and freshly ground black pepper (optional)

freshly chopped mint or coriander (cilantro), for sprinkling

cooked white rice or fresh naan bread, to serve

Mix the coconut milk, tomato purée (paste), garam masala, ginger, garlic, curry powder, curry paste, cayenne, turmeric and salt together in a bowl.

Oil the cooking dish of a 4.5 litre/8 pint/4 quart slow cooker. Put the onion in the cooking dish and top with the chicken.

Pour the coconut milk mixture over the chicken, completely covering the chicken. Top with butter. Cover and cook on High for 3–4 hours or on Low for 6–8 hours. Stir in the yogurt and cream and heat on Low for 15 minutes.

When ready to serve, taste and season with salt and pepper, if needed. Sprinkle with mint or coriander (cilantro) and serve with rice or naan bread.

CHICKEN & PEPPER CASSEROLE

Moroccan seasonings, savoury chicken, chickpeas and peppers come together to create a dish you will make again and again.

Serves 4-6

TO MARINATE THE CHICKEN

6 chicken thighs, bone in, trimmed of excess fat and skin

1 tsp salt

½ tsp very finely chopped garlic

¼ tsp freshly chopped root ginger

½ tsp ground cumin

½ tsp ground black pepper

2 small bay leaves

½ tbsp smoked paprika

FOR THE CASSEROLE

225 g/8 oz/1 cup canned chopped tomatoes

2 tbsp olive oil

1 medium onion, sliced

1 tsp each ground coriander, ground cumin and
very freshly chopped root ginger

3 tsp very finely chopped garlic

½ tsp cayenne pepper

salt, to taste

200 ml/7 fl oz/¾ cup chicken stock

1 large red pepper, deseeded and sliced

425 g/15 oz/2⅔ cups canned chickpeas, rinsed and drained

100 g/3½ oz/½ cup capers

Place the chicken thighs in a bowl and add the salt, garlic, ginger, cumin, black pepper, bay leaves and smoked paprika. Mix until the chicken is well coated, then cover and leave to marinate in the refrigerator for 30 minutes.

When ready to cook, place the tomatoes in the cooking dish of a 4.5 litre/8 pint/4 quart slow cooker. Heat the oil in a frying pan, add the chicken and brown for about 3–5 minutes until the chicken is golden. Remove and place in the cooking dish. Drain any excess oil from the pan.

Add the onion, spices and salt to the frying pan and stir for 1–2 minutes, just until the flavours come together and it is fragrant.

Stir in the stock, heating and scraping up the browned bits from the bottom of the pan to deglaze. Add to the cooking dish with the red pepper, chickpeas and capers. Cover and cook on High for 3–4 hours or on Low for 6–8 hours.

RED THAI DUCK CURRY

This rich spicy curry is even better eaten the next day. If time permits, cook it the day before you intend to eat it to let the flavours develop.

Serves 6

3 boneless duck breasts, skin on

2 tsp olive oil

4 tbsp Thai red curry paste

1 tbsp soft brown sugar

2 tbsp fish sauce

400 ml/14 fl oz/1⅔ cups canned coconut milk

2.5 cm/1 inch piece fresh root ginger, peeled and grated

1 lemongrass stem, bruised

2 kaffir lime leaves

½ whole red onion, peeled and sliced

1 green or red pepper, cored and sliced

150 g/5 oz/1 cup grape tomatoes

½ whole pineapple, cut into chunks

juice of ½ lime

Rinse the duck well and pat dry. Heat the oil in a frying pan over a medium heat, add the duck breasts, skin-side down, and brown well. Flip and brown the other side. Remove from the pan and slice. Discard the fat.

Place the duck in the cooking dish of a 4.5–7 litre/8–12 pint/4–6 quart slow cooker. Combine the curry paste, sugar and fish sauce in a bowl. Stir in the coconut milk and ginger, then pour over the duck. Add the lemongrass, lime leaves, red onion, pepper, tomatoes and pineapple to the dish. Cover and cook on Low for 6–8 hours. Stir in the lime juice and serve.

VEGGIES & VEGETARIAN

THREE BEAN TAGINE

Enjoy this delicious vegetarian three-bean tagine served over couscous, with flatbread, or topped with poached eggs.

Serves 4

few saffron strands

2–3 tbsp olive oil

1 small aubergine (eggplant), diced

1 onion, peeled and chopped

350 g/12 oz sweet potatoes, peeled and diced

225 g/8 oz carrots, peeled and chopped

1 cinnamon stick, bruised

1½ tsp ground cumin

salt and freshly ground black pepper

600 ml/1 pint/2½ cups vegetable stock

2 fresh mint sprigs

200 g/7 oz/1¼ cups canned red kidney beans, drained and rinsed

300 g/10 oz/1¼ cups canned haricot beans, drained

300 g/10 oz/1¼ cups canned flageolet beans, drained

1 tbsp freshly chopped mint, to garnish

Place warm water into a small bowl and sprinkle with the saffron strands. Leave to infuse for at least 10 minutes.

Heat the oil in a large, heavy-based saucepan, add the aubergine (eggplant) and onion and fry for 5 minutes before adding the sweet potatoes, carrots, cinnamon stick and ground cumin. Cook, stirring, until the vegetables are lightly coated in the cumin. Add the saffron with the soaking liquid and season to taste with salt and pepper.

Pour in the stock and add the mint sprigs. Rinse the beans, add to the pan and bring to the boil. Carefully transfer to the cooking dish of a 4.5 litre/8 pint/4 quart slow cooker. Cover and cook on Low for 6 hours, or until the vegetables are tender.

Adjust the seasoning to taste as needed before serving sprinkled with mint.

RATATOUILLE

Aubergine (eggplant), summer squash, peppers, tomatoes and lots of garlic are slow-cooked until meltingly tender. Serve with grilled (broiled) fish or meat, spoon onto toasted bread or even toss with freshly cooked pasta for an easy summer meal.

Serves 8–10

4 tbsp olive oil, plus extra for drizzling

2 medium onions, peeled and diced

½ tsp fine salt, plus extra for seasoning

450 g/1 lb aubergine (eggplant)

450 g/1 lb courgette (zucchini) or summer squash

2 large red, green, or yellow peppers (about 450 g/1 lb)

450 g/1 lb tomatoes

4 garlic cloves, peeled

2 tbsp tomato purée (paste)

25 g/1 oz/¼ cup freshly chopped basil leaves

Heat 2 tablespoons of the oil in a large frying pan over a medium heat until shimmering. Add the onions and season with salt. Cook for 30 minutes, stirring occasionally, until completely softened and light golden brown.

Meanwhile, prepare the rest of the vegetables. Trim the aubergine (eggplant) and courgette (zucchini), cut into 2.5 cm/1 inch cubes, and place in the cooking dish of a 7 litre/12 pint/6 quart slow cooker.

Trim, core and cut the peppers into 2.5 cm/1 inch dice and add to the cooking dish. Core the tomatoes, cut into 4 cm/1½ inch dice and add to the cooking dish. Finely chop the garlic and add to the dish.

When the onions are ready, add the tomato purée (paste) to the pan and stir to coat the onions. Transfer the onion mixture to the slow cooker. Add the remaining oil and the ½ teaspoon salt and stir to coat all the vegetables.

Cover and cook on High for 3–4 hours or on Low for 6–8 hours. If there is too much liquid for your taste, uncover for the last 30 minutes.

Stir in the basil and taste for seasoning, adding more salt as needed. Drizzle with extra olive oil before serving, if desired.

MIXED VEGETABLE CURRY

This curry has amazing colour and taste. It goes well with rice , roti, chapati or any other kind of flatbread.

Serves 4-6

2 tbsp vegetable oil

1 tsp cumin seeds

1 tsp black mustard seeds

2–3 garlic cloves, peeled and chopped

1 tbsp hot curry powder

2 onions, peeled and cut into wedges

1 large red pepper, deseeded and chopped

450 g/1 lb potatoes (or half potatoes, half sweet potatoes), peeled and chopped

175 g/6 oz carrots, peeled and chopped

175 g/6 oz cauliflower florets

300 ml/½ pint/1¼ cups water

125 g/4 oz/scant 1 cup frozen peas, thawed (optional)

3 tomatoes, chopped

few fresh curry leaves, chopped

2 tbsp ground almonds

4 tbsp plain yogurt

1 tbsp freshly chopped coriander (cilantro), to garnish

Heat the oil in a large frying pan, add the seeds and fry for 30 seconds, or until they pop. Add the garlic, curry powder and onions and cook gently for 5 minutes, or until the onions have softened.

Add the remaining vegetables, except for the peas and tomatoes, to the pan. Add the water, bring to the boil, then carefully transfer to the cooking dish of a 4.5 litre/8 pint/4 quart slow cooker.

Cover and cook on High for 3–3½ hours or on Low for 6–7 hours.

Add the peas, if using, and tomatoes and continue to cook on Low for 1 hour. Stir in the curry leaves, ground almonds and yogurt. Continue to cook on Low for 30 minutes, or until hot. Garnish with chopped coriander (cilantro) and serve.

VEGETABLE RISOTTO

Soft, creamy risotto dotted with vegetables and flavoured with Parmesan without standing over the stove. Serve as a side dish or as a main dish with a salad.

Serves 4

200 g/7 oz/1 cup Arborio rice

½ medium red pepper, diced

½ bunch spring onions (scallions), thinly sliced

1 green jalapeño pepper, deseeded and diced

4 tbsp butter or olive oil

1 garlic clove, peeled and chopped

600 ml/1 pint/2½ cups chicken stock

75 g/3 oz/¾ cup grated Parmesan cheese or vegetarian Italian hard cheese

125 ml/4 fl oz/½ cup single (half and half) cream

TO GARNISH

shaved Parmesan cheese or vegetarian Italian hard cheese, to taste

cracked black pepper, to taste

Place the rice, red pepper, spring onions (scallions), jalapeño pepper, butter and garlic in the cooking dish of a 2.2–3.4 litre/4–6 pint/2–3 quart slow cooker.

Pour in the stock and mix again. Cover and cook on High for 2½ hours or on Low for 5 hours.

Before serving fold in the cheese and cream. Top with the shaved cheese and cracked black pepper.

VEGETABLE & LENTIL CASSEROLE

This casserole is packed with squash, carrots, peppers and lentils to make a comforting dish that will warm you up when it's cold outside.

Serves 4

225 g/8 oz/generous 1 cup Puy lentils

1–2 tbsp olive oil

1 onion, peeled and chopped

2–3 garlic cloves, peeled and crushed

300 g/11 oz carrots, peeled and cut into chunks

3 celery stalks, sliced

350 g/12 oz/2½ cups butternut squash, peeled, deseeded and diced

1 litre/1¾ pints/4 cups vegetable stock

salt and freshly ground black pepper

few fresh oregano sprigs, plus extra to garnish

1 large red or orange pepper, deseeded and chopped

2 courgettes (zucchini), sliced (optional)

freshly chopped, or sprigs of, flat-leaf parsley, to garnish

150 ml/¼ pint/⅔ cup sour cream, to serve

Pour the lentils out onto a plate and look through them for any small stones, then rinse the lentils and reserve.

Heat the oil in a deep frying pan, add the onion, garlic, carrots and celery and sauté for 5 minutes, stirring occasionally. Add the squash and lentils. Pour in the stock and season to taste with salt and pepper. Add the oregano sprigs and bring to the boil. Carefully transfer to the cooking dish of a 4.5 litre/8 pint/4 quart slow cooker. Cover and cook on Low for 6 hours.

Add the pepper and courgettes (zucchini), if using, and stir. Continue to cook on Low for a further 1–2 hours until all the vegetables are tender. Adjust the seasoning, garnish with fresh parsley and serve with sour cream.

CAULIFLOWER & POTATO CURRY

Cauliflower and potato, a favourite combination of vegetables in India, unites cumin, turmeric and chili (red pepper) flakes. Fresh coriander (cilantro) provides a herbal note. Serve as a generous side dish or as a meatless main dish.

Serves 8

1 large cauliflower, cut into 2.5 cm/1 inch pieces

1 large Russet potato, peeled and cut into 2.5 cm/1 inch pieces

1 onion, peeled and diced

1 tomato, diced

5 cm/2 inch piece fresh root ginger, peeled and grated

2 garlic cloves, peeled and very finely chopped

2 jalapeño peppers, deseeded and sliced

1 tbsp cumin seeds

pinch cayenne pepper, or more to taste

1 tbsp garam masala

1 tbsp salt

1 tsp ground turmeric

3 tbsp vegetable oil

1 heaped tbsp freshly chopped coriander (cilantro)

Combine all the ingredients, except the coriander (cilantro), in the cooking dish of a 4.5 litre/8 pint/4 quart slow cooker and mix well.

Cover and cook on Low for 4 hours, stirring once or twice if possible.

Serve garnished with coriander.

VEGETABLE & COCONUT POT

Easy vegan Thai-inspired dish with coconut milk, plenty of garlic and lots of veggies. Comfort food at its best!

Serves 4-6

2 tbsp vegetable oil (or ghee for non-vegans)

1 tsp cumin seeds

1 cinnamon stick, bruised

3 whole cloves

3 cardamom pods, bruised

½–1 tsp chili powder

8 shallots, peeled and halved

2–3 garlic cloves, peeled and finely chopped

225 g/8 oz potatoes, peeled and cut into chunks

about 350 g/12 oz butternut squash, peeled, deseeded and cut into chunks

225 g/8 oz carrots, peeled and chopped

200 ml/7 fl oz/¾ cup water

300 ml/½ pint/1¼ cups coconut milk

225 g/8 oz French beans, trimmed and chopped

125 g/4 oz/scant 1 cup frozen peas, thawed

Heat the oil or ghee in a large saucepan, add the cumin seeds, cinnamon stick, cloves, cardamom pods and chili powder and fry for 30 seconds, or until the seeds pop.

Add the shallots, garlic, potatoes, squash and carrots and stir until the vegetables are coated in the flavoured oil. Add the water, bring to the boil, then carefully transfer to the cooking dish of a 4.5 litre/8 pint/4 quart slow cooker. Cover and cook on Low for 6 hours.

Pour in the coconut milk and add the chopped beans and peas. Stir gently until mixed and continue to cook on Low for a further 2 hours, or until the vegetables are tender. Serve.

STUFFED PEPPERS

Tender peppers filled with quinoa and Italian seasonings and slow-cooked in flavourful marinara sauce. Keep as it is or top with grated mozzarella.

Serves 6

550 g/1 lb 3 oz/3 cups cooked quinoa

1½ onions, peeled and diced

50 g/2 oz/1 cup sun-dried tomatoes, diced

2 tbsp olive oil

1 tbsp Italian seasoning

salt and freshly ground black pepper

6 peppers – any colours, trimmed, halved and deseeded

900 ml/1½ pints/3¾ cups tomato pasta sauce or marinara sauce

Mix the cooked quinoa, onion, sun-dried tomatoes, oil, Italian seasoning and salt and pepper together in bowl.

Place the pepper halves in the cooking dish of a 4.5–7 litre/8–12 pint/4–6 quart slow cooker and stuff each pepper with quinoa mixture. Pour the pasta sauce over the peppers. Cover and cook on Low for 6 hours.

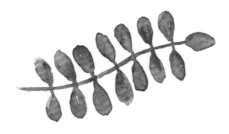

RED LENTIL DHAL

Dhal, a traditional Indian lentil dish, utilizes flavourful spices and aromatics to transform basic ingredients into a complex and delectable dish. Enjoy this version of dhal with brown rice, couscous or naan bread for a balanced and satisfying vegetarian meal.

Serves 6

1 tbsp olive oil

1 onion, peeled and diced

4 garlic cloves, peeled and very finely chopped

2 tbsp freshly grated root ginger

375 g/13 oz/2 cups dried red or yellow lentils, sorted and rinsed

1 tbsp garam masala

1 tbsp curry powder

1 tsp ground cumin

1 tsp ground coriander

1 tsp mustard powder

1 tsp ground turmeric

1 litre/1¾ pints/4 cups vegetable stock

425 g/15 oz/2 cups canned whole tomatoes, crushed with hands

150 g/5 oz baby spinach (optional)

freshly chopped coriander (cilantro) or parsley, for sprinkling

Heat the oil in a frying pan over a medium heat, add the onion, garlic and ginger and sauté for 5 minutes until the onion is softened.

Add the sautéed onion mixture, lentils, all the spices, stock and tomatoes into the cooking dish of a 4.5 litre/8 pint/4 quart slow cooker and stir.

Cover and cook on High for 3–4 hours or on Low for 6–8 hours.

If using, during the last 5 minutes of cooking, stir in the baby spinach and allow to wilt. To serve, sprinkle with coriander (cilantro) or parsley.

CHANA MASALA

This simplified version of an Indian favourite is a delightful way to showcase tasty chickpeas, onion, tomato, ginger and aromatic spices.

Serves 6

2 tbsp olive oil

1 onion, peeled and diced

3 garlic cloves, peeled and very finely chopped

1 tbsp freshly chopped root ginger, or ½ tsp ground ginger

3 cardamom pods, seeds removed and crushed (throw away the husks),
  or ¼ tsp ground cardamom

2 tsp ground cumin

1 tsp garam masala

½ tsp ground coriander

⅛ tsp cayenne pepper

¾ tsp salt, or more to taste

700 g/1½ lb/3½ cups canned whole peeled tomatoes with juice

850 g/1 lb 14 oz/5⅓ cups canned chickpeas, drained and rinsed

freshly chopped coriander (cilantro) or flat-leaf parsley, for sprinkling

Heat the oil in a frying pan over a medium heat, add the onion and cook for 7–8 minutes, stirring occasionally, until translucent and golden. Add the garlic and sauté, stirring, for 1 minute. Add the ginger, spices and the salt and stir constantly for about 30 seconds to toast the spices. Pour in the tomatoes and stir.

Pour the tomato and onion mixture into the cooking dish of a 4.5 litre/8 pint/4 quart slow cooker. Add the chickpeas and stir. Cover and cook on High for 3–4 hours or on Low for 6–8 hours. Taste and add more salt if desired. Serve sprinkled with coriander (cilantro) or parsley.

THREE SISTERS STEW

Three Sisters Stew is a fantastic dish with the Native American 'three sisters' of pumpkin or squash, beans and corn.

Serves 8-10

1 small sugar pumpkin or 1 large butternut squash, about 900 g/2 lb, cut into
   2.5 cm/1 inch cubes

2 tbsp olive oil

1 onion, peeled and chopped

4 garlic cloves, peeled and very finely chopped

1 green or red pepper, diced

425 g/15 oz/2 cups canned chopped tomatoes with juice

450 g/1 lb/3 cups cooked or canned pinto beans, drained and rinsed

325 g/11½ oz/2 cups sweetcorn kernels, from 2 large or 3 medium corn-on-the-
   cobs, or frozen and thawed

250 ml/8 fl oz/1 cup vegetable stock

1–2 small fresh hot chilies, deseeded and very finely chopped

2 tsp ground cumin

2 tsp chili powder, or to taste

1 tsp dried oregano

salt and freshly ground black pepper

15 g/½ oz/¼ cup freshly chopped coriander (cilantro) or parsley, to garnish

Stir all the ingredients in the cooking dish of a 6–7 litre/10½–12 pint/5–6 quart slow cooker.

Cover and cook on High for 4 hours or on Low for 8 hours.

Garnish with coriander (cilantro) before serving.

VEGETARIAN CHILI

An unbelievably easy, protein-rich and hearty chili to warm up the coldest of winter nights. Add crushed chili (red pepper) flakes if you like your chili with more heat.

Serves 6

1.2 kg/2¾ lb/4½ cups canned black beans, drained and rinsed

1 onion, peeled and diced

2 red peppers, diced

250 ml/8 fl oz/1 cup vegetable stock

75 g/3 oz/½ cup bulgur wheat

850 g/1 lb 14 oz/scant 4¼ cups canned chopped tomatoes

1 tsp ground cumin

1 tsp dried oregano

1 tsp chili powder

¼ tsp cayenne pepper

freshly chopped coriander (cilantro), to garnish

Place all the ingredients into the cooking dish of a 4.5 litre/8 pint/4 quart slow cooker and stir.

Cover and cook on High for 4–4½ hours or on Low for 8–9 hours.

Serve with rice and garnish with coriander (cilantro).

MEXICAN BEAN STEW

This hearty, slow-cooked stew with south-of-the-border flavours features beans and spices to make a satisfying, warming stew.

Serves 8

1 litre/1¾ pints/4 cups vegetable stock

425 g/15 oz/about 1½ cups canned black-eyed beans, drained and rinsed

425 g/15 oz/about 1½ cups canned kidney beans, drained and rinsed

425 g/15 oz/about 1½ cups canned white beans, drained and rinsed

425 g/15 oz/2 cups canned chopped tomatoes

1 large onion, peeled and chopped

1 yellow or red pepper, diced

1 jalapeño pepper, deseeded and finely diced, add more or less to taste

3 garlic cloves, peeled and very finely chopped

2 tbsp tomato purée (paste)

1 tbsp Mexican oregano or regular oregano

1 tbsp medium (regular) chili powder

1 tsp ground cumin

¼–½ tsp chipotle chili powder, or, for smokiness without heat, use smoked paprika

salt and freshly ground black pepper

Combine all the ingredients in the cooking dish of a 4.5–7 litre/8–12 pint/4–6 quart slow cooker.

Cover and cook on High for 4–6 hours or on Low for 8 hours.

DESSERTS, TREATS & PRESERVES

CHEESECAKE WITH RASPBERRIES

You can make luscious, silky cheesecakes with the help of a slow cooker water bath.

Serves 8

vegetable oil, for greasing

250 ml/8 fl oz/1 cup warm water, for the water bath

1 lemon

350 g/12 oz/1½ cups cream cheese or Neufchatel, softened

100 g/3½ oz/½ cup granulated sugar

1 tbsp flour or ½ tbsp cornflour (cornstarch)

1 tsp vanilla extract

3 medium (large) eggs, lightly whisked

TO DECORATE

125 g/4 oz/1 cup raspberries

50 g/2 oz/½ cup digestive biscuit (graham) crumbs

Lightly oil a 1.1–1.7 litre/2–3 pint/1–1½ quart soufflé dish. Be sure the dish fits into the cooking dish of a 4.5–7 litre/8–12 pint/4–6 quart slow cooker. Line the bottom of the soufflé dish with baking parchment. Cut a 69 x 46 cm/27 x 18 inch piece of heavy foil in half lengthways and cut along the fold line. Fold the halves lengthways into thirds. Criss-cross strips on the work surface and place the baking parchment lined baking dish on top of the foil strips. These will be the handles that will help lift the soufflé dish in and out of the slow cooker.

Pour the warm water into the cooking dish of the slow cooker.

Finely grate the lemon zest and reserve. Squeeze the lemon and reserve 2 tablespoons of lemon juice. Beat the cream cheese in a bowl for 1 minute. Scrape down the bowl and add the sugar, flour and vanilla and beat until combined. Beat in the eggs, lemon juice and zest and beat until very smooth, scraping the bowl as needed. Pour the cream cheese mixture into the prepared soufflé dish and cover tightly with more foil. Using the strips and keeping the dish even so as not to slosh the mixture, set the dish into the cooking dish of the slow cooker. Leave the strips in place under the dish.

Cover and cook on High for 2½ hours, or until the centre of the cheesecake is set. Use the foil strips to carefully remove the soufflé dish from the slow cooker. Uncover and cool on a wire rack. Cover and chill in the refrigerator for at least 4 hours or up to 24 hours.

To serve, top with raspberries and a sprinkling of crushed biscuit (graham) crumbs.

POACHED PEARS

Poached pears make a great dessert on their own, but my favourite use for them is as an ingredient in baked goods. Poaching the pears before using them in quick breads, muffins, cakes and pies gives them vibrant, spicy flavour and ensures that they won't be undercooked.

Serves 8

250 ml/8 fl oz/1 cup apple juice
4 large (or 8 small) firm cooking pears, skin peeled, bottom cut flat (so pears will stand up straight when served), and with stems on (this looks pretty but also makes them much easier to handle with tongs)
2 cinnamon sticks
thinly pared zest from 1 lemon

Pour the apple juice into the bottom of the cooking dish of a 4–4.5 litre/7–8 pint/3½–4 quart slow cooker. Lay the pears on their sides in the juice, then add the cinnamon sticks and half of the lemon zest.

Cover and cook on High for 1 hour or on Low for 2 hours, turning the pears to their other side halfway through the cooking time. Remove the pears from the slow cooker and reserve.

Pour the juice from the slow cooker through a sieve (strainer) into a saucepan. Add the cinnamon sticks and bring to the boil over a medium-high heat. Boil for about 15 minutes, until it is reduced by about one-third and is a thin syrup consistency. Remove from the heat and stir in the remaining lemon zest.

To serve, place the pears on plates (half of a large pear or 1 whole small pear), then ladle the syrup over them.

NUTTY CARROT CAKE

I love coming home to a delicious dinner waiting in the slow cooker, but having a dessert waiting is even better!

Serves 16

300 g/11 oz/1¼ cups unsweetened apple purée (applesauce)

400 g/14 oz/2 cups granulated sugar

3 medium (large) eggs, room temperature

250 g/9 oz/2 cups plain (all-purpose) flour

1 tsp bicarbonate of soda (baking soda)

1½ tsp baking powder

½ tsp salt

1 tsp ground cinnamon

4 carrots, peeled and grated

175 g/6 oz/1 cup shredded sweetened coconut

100 g/3½ oz/1 cup chopped nuts, such as pecans or walnuts (optional)

1 tsp vanilla extract

225 g/8 oz canned crushed pineapple, undrained

toasted coconut or chopped toasted nuts, to decorate (optional)

FOR THE FROSTING

125 g/4 oz/½ cup butter, room temperature

225 g/8 oz/1 cup cream cheese, room temperature

1 tsp vanilla extract

450 g/1 lb/4½ cups icing (confectioners') sugar

For the cake, line the cooking dish of a 4.5 litre/8 pint/4 quart slow cooker with 2 pieces of foil perpendicular to each other, making sure there is enough foil overhanging the edges of the slow cooker. These will be your handles later. Oil the foil.

Whisk the apple purée (applesauce), sugar and eggs together. Whisk in the flour, bicarbonate of soda (baking soda), baking powder, salt and cinnamon. Stir in the carrots, coconut, nuts, vanilla extract and pineapple. Gently pour the batter into the prepared cooking dish.

Cover the dish with several folded absorbent paper towels or a clean dish towel and place the lid on top. This will absorb some of the steam and keep it from dripping back onto the cake. Cook on Low for 2¾–3¼ hours. If your slow cooker heats unevenly, rotate the insert 90 degrees every 30 minutes.

Test the cake by inserting a toothpick into the centre. If it comes out clean, the cake is done. The cake should be slightly domed when cooked. Remove the cooking dish, place on a wire rack and allow the cake to cool for 30 minutes, then use the foil sling to lift the cake out of the dish and place on a wire rack. Gently remove the foil from the cake and let the cake cool completely.

To make the frosting, beat the butter and cream cheese together in a bowl until fluffy. Add the vanilla and sugar and beat until smooth. Cut the cold cake into layers if desired, then frost. Top with toasted coconut or chopped toasted nuts, if desired.

CARAMEL BREAD PUDDING

Bread pudding makes a fantastic dessert and is a wonderful way to use up leftover bread.

Serves 8–10

vegetable oil, for greasing

450 g/1 lb challah or brioche loaf, slightly stale, cut into cubes

750 ml/1¼ pints/3 cups milk, or almond or coconut milk

4 medium (large) eggs, lightly beaten

50 g/2 oz/¼ cup light brown sugar

1 tsp vanilla extract

¼ tsp salt

FOR THE SALTED CARAMEL SAUCE

150 g/5 oz/¾ cup brown sugar

125 ml/4 fl oz/½ cup double (heavy) cream

125 g/4 oz/½ cup butter

2 tbsp golden syrup (light corn syrup)

1 tsp vanilla extract; ½ tsp sea salt

Oil a cooking dish of a 4–4.5 litre/7–8 pint/3½–4 quart slow cooker. Place the bread cubes in the cooking dish. Whisk the milk, eggs, sugar, vanilla and salt together, then pour over the bread cubes. Press the bread cubes down in the egg mixture, making sure they are all moistened. Cover and cook on Low for 3–3½ hours until a knife comes out clean. Turn off the cooker and allow to stand for a further 30 minutes.

To make the salted caramel sauce, gently bring the sugar, cream, butter and syrup to the boil over a medium heat, then reduce the heat and simmer for 3 minutes. Take off the heat and stir in the vanilla and salt. Serve the pudding with the sauce.

LEMON POPPY SEED CAKE

This is a moist and delicious lemon cake bursting with nutty poppy seeds.

Serves 12

vegetable oil, for greasing

250 ml/8 fl oz/1 cup buttermilk, or 250 ml/8 fl oz/1 cup milk mixed with 1 tsp lemon juice

1 medium (large) egg

3 tbsp butter, melted

1 tsp vanilla extract

½ tsp lemon extract

185 g/6½ oz/1½ cups plain (all-purpose) flour

100 g/3½ oz/½ cup granulated sugar

40 g/1½ oz/¼ cup cornmeal

1 tbsp poppy seeds

1 tsp bicarbonate of soda (baking soda)

1 tsp finely chopped lemon zest; ½ tsp salt

OPTIONAL ICING

100 g/3½ oz/1 cup icing (confectioners') sugar

¼ tsp vanilla extract

1 tbsp milk, plus extra if needed

Lightly oil the cooking dish of a 4–4.5 litre/7–8 pint/3½–4 quart slow cooker. Use the foil sling method for easy removal from the slow cooker insert (*see* page 196): 2 pieces of foil, perpendicular and long enough to use as handles to lift the cake out. Oil the foil.

Whisk the buttermilk, egg, melted butter, vanilla and lemon extracts together in a bowl. Add the remaining ingredients and mix together until just combined and smooth.

Pour the batter into the prepared cooking dish. Cover and cook on Low for 2¼–2¾ hours until the internal temperature is 93°C/200°F and the centre appears set, rotating the cooking dish halfway through the cooking time to cook the cake evenly.

When the cake is cooked through, place the cooking dish on a wire rack for 30 minutes. Loosen the edges of the cake and remove from the dish using the foil. Allow to cool completely.

To make the icing, mix the icing (confectioners') sugar, vanilla and milk together. Add a little more milk if the icing is too thick to drizzle on the cake.

PEACH & BLUEBERRY COBBLER

Fruit cobbler is especially wonderful in the summer when so many fruits are available. This peach blueberry cobbler doesn't disappoint, and there is no need to heat up the kitchen by turning on the oven.

Serves 8

vegetable oil, for greasing

650 g/1lb 7 oz/3 cups peach slices,
    fresh or frozen and thawed

125 g/4 oz/1 cup blueberries,
    fresh or frozen and thawed

2 tbsp cornflour (cornstarch)

50 g/2 oz/¼ cup light brown sugar

FOR THE COBBLER TOPPING

125 g/4 oz/1 cup plain
    (all-purpose) flour

200 g/7 oz/1 cup granulated sugar

1 tbsp baking powder

½ tsp ground cinnamon

¼ tsp salt

65 g/2½ oz/5 tbsp butter

250 ml/8 fl oz/1 cup milk

Oil the cooking dish of a 4.5 litre/8 pint/4 quart slow cooker liberally with oil spray (or it can be greased with unsalted butter). Add the peaches and blueberries and toss with the cornflour (cornstarch). Sprinkle with the brown sugar.

For the topping, stir the flour, sugar, baking powder, cinnamon and salt together in a bowl. Using 2 knives, cut the butter into the flour until the mixture resembles breadcrumbs, then stir in the milk until combined. Spoon the batter over the fruit.

Cover the cooking dish with absorbent paper towels or a clean dish towel and place the lid on top. This keeps condensation from the cobbler dripping onto the cake. Cook on High for 3 hours. Remove the towel(s) and cook for a further 30 minutes before serving.

CINNAMON PECAN CAKE

This cake is moist, flavourful and easy to make. It's perfect for special occasions and weekend mornings with a cup of tea or coffee.

Serves 12

225 g/8 oz/1 cup sour cream

125 ml/4 fl oz/½ cup milk

1 medium (large) egg

3 tbsp melted butter or oil

1 tsp vanilla extract

225 g/8 oz/1¾ cups plain (all-purpose) flour

100 g/3½ oz/½ cup granulated sugar

1 tsp bicarbonate of soda (baking soda)

1 tsp ground cinnamon

½ tsp salt

50 g/2 oz/½ cup pecans, toasted and chopped

Lightly oil the cooking dish of a 4–4.5 litre/7–8 pint/3½–4 quart slow cooker. Use the foil sling method for easy removal from the slow cooker insert (*see* page 196): 2 pieces of foil, perpendicular and long enough to use as handles to lift the cake out. Oil the foil.

Whisk the wet ingredients together in a large bowl. In another bowl, mix together all the dry ingredients, except the pecans, then stir the dry and wet ingredients together until combined. Stir in the pecans.

Pour the batter into the prepared cooking dish and smooth the top. Cover and cook on Low 2¼–2¾ hours until cooked through. Rotate the dish halfway through cooking if your slow cooker does not heat evenly.

When the cake is cooked through, place the cooking dish on a wire rack for
30 minutes. Loosen the edges of the cake and remove from the dish using the foil.
Allow to cool completely.

Note:

To bake in a loaf tin, pour the batter in an oiled loaf pan that fits into a 7 litre/12 pint/6 quart
slow cooker. Bake as above or until cooked through.

BLACKBERRY CRUMBLE

Sweet blackberries topped with a crisp crumble is even better topped with some vanilla ice cream or a dollop of whipped cream.

Serves 8-10

vegetable oil, for greasing

FOR THE TOPPING

100 g/3½ oz.¾ cup plain (all purpose) flour

65 g/2½ oz/¾ cup rolled oats

50 g/2 oz/¼ cup plus 2 tbsp light brown sugar

1 tsp ground cinnamon

¼ tsp salt

6 tbsp cold unsalted butter

FOR THE FILLING

50 g/2 oz/¼ cup granulated sugar

2 tbsp cornflour (cornstarch)

650 g/1 lb 7 oz/5 cups frozen blackberries, fresh or frozen

1 tbsp lemon juice

Whisk the flour, oats, brown sugar, cinnamon and salt together in a large bowl. Dice the butter into small chunks and add to the mixture, cutting it in with 2 knives or a pastry cutter until the mixture is crumbly. Set aside.

For the filling, stir the granulated sugar and cornflour (cornstarch) together in a bowl. Oil the cooking dish of a 7 litre/12 pint/6 quart slow cooker. Put the blackberries and lemon juice into the cooking dish, sprinkle with the sugar mixture and stir.

Sprinkle the topping mix over the berries. Place absorbent paper towels or a clean dish towel over the slow cooker and cover with the lid. Cook on High for 2½–3 hours until the top is cooked and the fruit is bubbly.

NUT-STUFFED BAKED APPLES

Nothing says 'autumn' like the fragrance and flavour of cooked apples, especially when they're spiced with cinnamon.

Serves 4

50 g/2 oz/¼ cup walnuts, coarsely chopped

3 tbsp dried currants or raisins

225 g/8 oz/1 cup (packed) soft brown sugar, plus an extra 2½ tbsp

¾ tsp ground cinnamon

¼ tsp ground nutmeg

4 medium cooking apples, cored

200 ml/7 fl oz/¾ cup cider

Combine the walnuts, currants and 2½ tablespoons brown sugar in a small bowl. Add ¼ teaspoon of the ground cinnamon, stirring to combine. Peel the top third of each apple and place the apples in the cooking dish of a 4.5 litre/8 pint/4 quart slow cooker. Spoon the walnut mixture into the cavity of each apple.

Combine the remaining cinnamon and the nutmeg, brown sugar and cider in a small bowl and stir well. Pour over the apples.

Cover and cook on Low for 2½–3 hours until the apples are tender. Remove the apples with a slotted spoon and spoon 50 ml/2 fl oz/¼ cup cooking liquid over each serving.

UPSIDE DOWN PINEAPPLE CAKE

Pineapple and cherries caramelized with brown sugar make the top of this classic cake. If you don't have pineapple on hand, use sliced pears, plums or peaches instead.

Serves 8

5 tbsp unsalted butter, cut into small pieces, plus extra for greasing

175 g/6 oz/¾ cup firmly packed dark brown sugar

3 tbsp dark rum (optional)

8 canned pineapple rings

8 fresh, frozen or maraschino cherries, pitted and stems removed

100 g/3½ oz/¾ cup plain (all-purpose or cake) flour

125 g/4 oz/⅔ cup granulated sugar

¾ tsp baking powder

½ tsp ground cinnamon

¼ tsp ground nutmeg

¼ tsp salt

1 medium (large) egg, at room temperature

1 medium (large) egg yolk, at room temperature

2 tbsp milk

50 ml/2 fl oz/¼ cup reserved pineapple juice

Butter the inside of the cooking dish of a 4.5 litre/8 pint/4 quart slow cooker. Line completely with foil, then butter the foil. Switch to High. Sprinkle the butter pieces, brown sugar and rum over the foil on the bottom of the cooking dish, then arrange the pineapple slices over the top in a slightly overlapping ring pattern, placing one in the centre and pressing the pineapple into the sugar. Place a cherry in the centre of each pineapple ring.

Sift the flour, sugar, baking powder, cinnamon, nutmeg and salt together into a large bowl.

In a separate bowl, beat the egg, egg yolk, milk and pineapple juice together. Add the egg mixture to the dry ingredients and mix until just combined to make a smooth batter.

Pour the batter over the pineapple and smooth the top with a spatula. Lay absorbent paper towels or a clean dish towel over the top of the cooking dish and cover with the lid.

Cook on High for about 3½ hours until the cake begins to brown slightly on the sides and springs back when touched in the middle. Turn off the slow cooker and allow the cake to stand for about 30 minutes.

Using the foil, lift the cake from the cooking dish and place on the work surface for 30 minutes until cool. Carefully remove the foil and invert the cake onto a platter so you can see the caramelized pineapples.

BLACKCURRANT JAM

Making jam in a slow cooker means no more scorched fruit! You need to weigh your fruit and sugar to make jam. Use an equal weight of fruit and sugar.

Makes 1.1 litres/2 pints/4²/₃ cups

2 kg/4½ lb blackcurrants, or other fruits, washed and roughly chopped
granulated sugar, the same weight as the cleaned fruit
100 ml/3½ fl oz/⅓ cup lemon juice

Place all the ingredients into the cooking dish of a 4.5 litre/8 pint/4 quart slow cooker. Put a plate in the freezer.

Cover and cook on Low for 2½ hours, stirring once or twice throughout.

Uncover and cook on High for a further 3–4 hours until the jam starts to firm up to a thick consistency. You can test the consistency of the resulting jam by spooning a bit of the hot jam onto the cold plate in the freezer. The resulting texture of the cooled jam will show you if it is thick enough for your tastes or if it needs to cook a while longer.

When the jam is done, spoon into two 600 ml/1 pint jars or four 300 ml/10 fl oz jars, cover with a lid and store in the refrigerator for up to a month.

HOT CINNAMON APPLE CIDER

Cider can be mulled then held at a warm temperature until everyone is ready to grab a mugful straight from the slow cooker with no fuss.

Serves 8

1.7 litres/3 pints/7 cups cider

6 x 7.5-cm/3-inch long cinnamon sticks, plus extra for serving if desired

1 organic orange, scrubbed clean

2 tbsp whole cloves

1 whole allspice pod

rum of choice, to serve (optional)

Pour the cider into the cooking dish of a 2.2–3.4 litre/4–6 pint/2–3 quart slow cooker. Add the cinnamon sticks.

With a toothpick, poke holes all around the orange, about 1–2.5 cm/½–1 inch apart, then carefully poke cloves into the holes. Place the orange into the cider and add the allspice.

Cover and cook on Low for 4 hours until hot and fragrant. Ladle into mugs along with about 2 tablespoons rum, if using. Place a cinnamon stick in each glass if desired and serve.

INDEX

Entries with upper-case initials indicate recipes.

If you enjoyed this book please sign up for updates,
information and offers on further titles in this series at
www.flametreepublishing.com